OMG!
IT'S
HARVEY KORMAN'S
SON!

by
Chris Korman
with
Ron Brawer

BearManor Media

Orlando, Florida

OMG! It's Harvey Korman's Son!
© 2020 Chris Korman. All Rights Reserved.

No portion of this publication may be reproduced, stored, and/or copied electronically (except for academic use as a source), nor transmitted in any form or by any means without the prior written permission of the publisher and/or author.

Published in the USA by
BearManor Media
1317 Edgewater Dr. #110
Orlando, FL 32804
www.BearManorMedia.com

Softcover Edition
ISBN: 978-1-62933-618-3

Printed in the United States of America

Foreword
A Letter from Carol Burnett

Dear Chris,

By the time Spring, 1967 came around, my husband Joe Hamilton, as our producer (along with Bob Banner, our executive producer) was busy putting together our writing and production staff for *The Carol Burnett Show*, many of whom came out of *The Garry Moore Show* in New York and were willing to take a chance on Hollywood. At the same time, we were on a serious lookout for our very own gang of comedians who would play and have fun with us every week the way we did on Garry's show.

    Joe and I had been huge fans of *The Danny Kaye Show*, and particularly of his incredibly talented second banana, Harvey Korman. Harvey was to Danny what Carl Reiner was to Sid Cesar, and Art Carney was to Jackie Gleason. "Second Banana" is a term that has been used in comedy as far back as I can remember. It probably dates back to vaudeville. I never took to it much, though, because the good ones never fit into that "second" slot, as far as I was concerned. In fact, lots of times they were the ones who walked away with the laughs... if the star would allow it. Those stars I've mentioned weren't afraid to let their teammates score a touchdown. They knew it only made the show better overall.

The Danny Kaye Show went off the air in 1967 and we were premiering that fall. All I could think about was, *We need a Harvey Korman. We need a consummate actor with comedy chops to spare.*

The penny finally dropped, the light bulb lit up, and I came to the brilliant conclusion to actually ask THE Harvey Korman himself if he would work with us. Now that Danny's show would no longer be on, could we... would he...???

I believe we had a call in to his agent when one afternoon I happened to see Harvey himself headed for his car in the CBS parking lot at Television City.

He didn't notice me.

I thought about it for a nanosecond and then I shouted, "Harvey!"

He turned and smiled. We hardly knew each other. I waved, smiled back, and then proceeded to jump him.

I may be exaggerating, but I seem to remember leaning him back over a car hood.

"Please, please be on our show! You're the very best! PLEASE?"

It wasn't exactly the most professional way to offer someone a job, but it worked. Harvey signed on, and I was in heaven.

Carol

Foreword
A Letter from Peter Marshall

I've known Chris since he was a young boy, five or six years old. He was always the sweetest kid around. He loved baseball, and Harvey took him to almost every Dodgers home game. In fact, Harvey took Chris everywhere, and always dressed him to the nines.

As a child, Chris couldn't articulate and function like a typical child. I thought this was going to be his way of life, that he wouldn't be able to function well as an adult. But because of Harvey's devotion to his son, Chris turned out remarkably well.

Harvey was a wonderful father: He sent Chris, age five, to the Frostig Center for Learning Disabilities. From there, I watched Chris grow and develop into an amazing young man. I fondly remember when he graduated from Frostig and gave a speech; he verbally struggled a bit but he was so cute and bright, his speech was truly a marvelous event.

With the treatment and support Chris received from Frostig, with Harvey's unstinting help, and with Chris' innate drive to improve himself, Chris has become one of the most amazing adults I know. He's married with a child, he functions wonderfully and speaks beautifully.

Chris is one of my favorite people in the whole wide world.

Peter Marshall
(*Hollywood Squares*)

BACKSTORY

My mother was Donna Ray Ehlert. She was a model and etiquette instructor in Milwaukee, Wisconsin, back in the days when etiquette—manners—still actually mattered.

My father was Harvey Hershel Korman.

In 1959, a writer on TV's *The Red Skelton Show* wrote and directed a stage play in Chicago called Mr. and Mrs.

Mom and Dad were both cast in the production. They met, dated, fell in love, and, in 1960, got married.

I was born five years later—May 24, 1967, to be exact—in Cedars of Lebanon Hospital, Los Angeles, California.

At birth, I had hyaline membrane disease, which is a lack of oxygen to the brain and central nervous system. If it isn't caught and cleared within 72 hours, you can develop methemoglobinemia or blue baby syndrome. My case was caught, though not before it led to future problems, as we'll see.

Dad and me.

MY FATHER THE CHICKEN

In 1960, at Mom's urging, my parents moved to Los Angeles so Dad could better pursue an acting career.

After a year of struggle and disappointment, he was cast as Ken Carter in the film, Living Venus.

He did a guest appearance on *The Red Skelton Show*.

That led to three Munsters episodes, a Hazel, The Jack Benny Show, and, eventually, I Love Lucy.

Lucille Ball was a close friend of Carol Burnett, who had *The Carol Burnett Show* on CBS. Lucy adored Dad. She told Carol, "If you don't sign him, I will."

Carol signed him.

For the next ten years, he built an enormously successful career. Or, as Dad put it, "I got famous because I cross-dressed every other week."

The shows were taped in front of a live audience, two shows, one after the other, on Friday night, and aired over the following two weeks.

When I was four years old, Mom took my older sister Maria and me to the studio to watch the early taping.

I found it totally weird, totally disorienting to see my father on stage, dressed as a chicken, *puck-puck-pucking* around a fake barnyard, then, a week later, watching the same dad-as-a-chicken on our TV set, with the puck-puck- pucker sitting right next to me.

CHRIS GETS THE BOOT

My first school experience was in a Pre-K program at the Center for Early Education in West Hollywood, LA. Their website describes the place as "a socio-economically and culturally diverse independent school for children, toddler through grade six."

In truth, it was a school for "socio-economically and culturally diverse" children who had not been born with hyaline membrane disease.

It didn't go well.

The school psychologist recommended that I be tested.

CHRIS GETS TESTED

I was tested.
I had an LD.
A learning disability.

Surprise-surprise.

MY LD

Okay, if you yourself have a learning disability, you can skip this next part.

If this is new territory for you, please take a moment.

A learning disability is a neurological disorder. In simple terms, a learning disability results from a difference in the way a person's brain is "wired." Children with learning disabilities are as smart or smarter than their peers. But they may have difficulty reading, writing, spelling, reasoning, recalling and/or organizing information if left to figure things out by themselves or if taught in conventional ways.

http://www.ldonline.org/ldbasics/whatisld

In other words, we're different.

After a year at the Center for Early Education, I was very much aware of that fact.

My parents quickly grasped the situation, and emphasized to me that my differences were challenges, and that everyone else on the planet also had challenges.

I wasn't a weirdo; I had gross motor skill issues.

I was able to do things, I just did them at a slower pace.

My learning disability involved a delay in memory retention.

For example, let's say you—you being a "normal" person—read a page from a Young Adult novel like The Hunger Games and it took you two-and-half minutes to read and comprehend that page.

It would take me just over 7 minutes.

That's right; about three times longer to absorb that one page of information.

FYI: Albert Einstein didn't learn to read till he was nine years old; Walt Disney had trouble reading his entire life; Michael Phelps, Daniel

Radcliffe, Whoopi Goldberg, Charles Schwab, Jay Leno, Justin Timberlake, Anderson Cooper...

Well, you get the idea. Don't you?

THANK YOU, CAROL!
THANK YOU, CAROL

One of Dad's best friends was Ernie Anderson, who was the voice of ABC and *The Love Boat*. Ernie and his wife Edwina lived in the Valley with their young son Paul Thomas, who is now a film director.

When I was five or six years old, Ernie and Edwina used to throw extravagant parties, with lots of games and activities. For the kids, there was an Olympic-style relay race crossed with an obstacle course. Each team had to scamper over barricades, crawl through tubes, swing from a rope tied to a tree branch, wade through a pool of water, all kinds of crazy stuff.

Needless to say, I was not the most skilled child when it came to obstacle courses: My team invariably came in last, and I arrived last of the last.

One year, as I ran for the finish line, none other than Carol Burnett herself stood there, waiting for me. She stooped down, gave me a big hug, and patted me on the back.

"Nice going, Chris!" she said. "Excellent race!"

You understand, I'd seen her at the studio numerous times, before or after Dad taped one of the shows, but this was the first time she treated me in a personal manner.

It was a seminal moment in my life. She saw that I was struggling, that I needed validation, and she answered the call. My self-esteem went from zero straight into the stratosphere.

Now, some fifty years later, I still get goose bumps thinking about it.

THE FROSTIG SCHOOL

Our school was founded in 1951 by Marianne Frostig, Ph.D., who was a pioneer, leader and advocate in education for children with learning disabilities. In fact, she was helping children with learning disabilities before there was a medical term for this diagnosis.
    https://frostigschool.org/about/history/

    The Frostig School had a whole-child approach to education; they didn't just teach us reading, writing, and arithmetic, they appealed to our emotional, psychological, and physical needs, with a focus on our strengths.
    When I got there, I felt a surge of Oh my God, I'm around people like me, people who understand me, understand my struggles.
    I felt embraced; I felt here we are, all of us in the same boat.
    At the risk of redundancy: Having a learning disability entails a lot of High Anxiety. (Hi, Mel!) You wake up every morning scared shitless that at some point(s) during the day you're going to sound like a complete idiot and everyone is going to treat you like you are.

LIFE AT FROSTIG

The focus was always on what we do well and expanding from there. I had an hour of physical therapy every day.

To overcome an issue with depth perception, I learned and practiced a simple exercise: shut my eyes, and, with my hands apart, index finger pointing, try to touch those two fingertips.

Simple, right? (Try it.)

For my gross motor skills problem, there was a balance bar like gymnasts perform on, only this one was very low, barely off the ground. I'd walk on that with my eyes closed.

We also used medicine balls, those big inflated plastic orbs you see in gyms. The idea was to maintain your balance while sitting on one, or lying crosswise on your stomach, and either trying not to move at all or else keeping your balance while slowly rolling around.

For hand-eye co-ordination, there was volleyball, which I never really enjoyed.

At home, Dad and I spent many hours playing catch with a whiffle ball.

CHRIS GOES GOLFING

In 1972, my first year at Frostig, the board of trustees met with Dad and urged him to sponsor a school fundraiser.

I was impressed.

"Chris, it's no big deal. They want my name attached is all. The First Annual Harvey Korman Invitational Celebrity Golf Tournament."

"The first?"

"Exactly. If that's what they want, they should give me a break on the tuition."

"You gonna do it?"

"I guess. I mean, the Frostig's board will handle the arrangements. All I need to do is invite some celebrities. Then, at the actual event, I get on stage and introduce them, and say a few nice words about the school. Easy."

"Do you have to be funny?"

"I'm always funny. Hey, wanna sit up on stage with me?" "Okay, sure."

"Maybe even get up and say a few words about the school." "What? No!"

"Okay, no pressure."

I thought about it, about standing up on stage with Dad and talking about my Frostig experience. The more I thought about it, the more it sounded like fun.

"Okay, Dad, I'll do it!" "Great!"

Mom was less sanguine. She felt that the situation would be extremely stressful. And, really, what was the point of putting me through that? The audience was coming to see Dad and his celebrity friends, not to hear me stutter.

But at that point, I'd convinced myself that it would be a great experience, that I'd be the star of Frostig.

Of course, I had no notion of what I was getting myself into. What seemed, in the comforts of home, like a cool and exciting experience, became scarier and scarier as the tournament days drew closer.

A week away, I considered backing out; it was too late, everyone knew I was going to be part of the show.

The day of the event, I was a nervous wreck.

When I finally stood at the podium and peered out at the crowd, I was in such a state of panic that whatever words I was going to say went right out of mind. All I could manage was, "Hi, I'm Christopher Peter Korman and I'd like to introduce my dad, Harvey Korman."

When Dad got up and joined me, he raised my hand like a boxing referee holding up the champion's hand.

The audience went wild with applause. Yep, I loved it.

ONE BAD YEAR

For the next thirteen years, the Frostig Harvey Korman International Celebrity Golf Tournament became an annual event.

It was always held at the Westin Mission Hills Resort in Rancho Mirage, except for one year, when it was at Stouffer's Esmarelda, in Indian Wells, near Palm Springs.

That one was a nightmare. They hadn't finished constructing the place, so I have no idea what possessed the golf committee to decide that this venue would be fabulous.

There was no dining room yet; we had to take our meals in the parking lot, which was roped off with the yellow tape you see at crime scenes.

That first morning, when breakfast was set up, Dad was furious. He screamed to no one in particular, "A four-time Emmy Award winner—" (meaning himself) "and a Golden Globe winner—" (ditto) "has to eat fucking breakfast in the fucking parking lot? In the heat of fucking *Palm Springs*?"

FORE!

POSTER CHILD

Dad and I co-hosted the tourney for 13 years. Each year, it got easier for me to get up there and make my presentation.

I got to be known as the Frostig Poster Child.

Each year, as my confidence increased, my presentation evolved, even as it stayed simple and direct:

"Hi I'm Chris Korman, Harvey Korman's son, and this is what Frostig has done for me, for my development, how it helped me articulate my thoughts in a coherent manner, and this is what Frostig can do for your LD child. If you invest in the school, your children will have the opportunity to become high functioning adults and not look at their lives as an endless series of miserable days they have to struggle through."

Then I'd introduce the celebrities, sometimes with a joke or two. After the speeches and appeals, we hit the links.

Although I never actually played in any of the tournaments, over the years I got to be pretty decent at golf.

Well, decent at putting.

The driving range was another matter. To hit the ball straight you have to keep your head aligned with your body.

With my lack of hand-eye coordination, that was a huge challenge: If I moved my head one inch to the left, the ball zoomed hard-left; if I moved my head an inch to the right, the damn ball flew hard-right.

Many a golfer playing ahead had to duck for cover; the less-fortunate ones raised their fist and threatened retaliation.

The safest thing for the course director was to just give me a golf cart and pray that I wouldn't run anybody over.

Shuffling off to Florida.

CHRIS THE ATHLETE

Besides my annual golf misadventures, I often played tennis with Dad.

My parents had me take tennis lessons at eight or nine years old. Tennis was even better than whiffle ball at developing hand-eye co-ordination and depth perception. I got to love the sport and, eventually, to be pretty decent at it.

Dad was a terrific tennis player, though he would insist that he was just okay.

I also loved the trampoline. Great fun, bouncing up and down. Twice a week I went to a day camp in Santa Monica run by Mike Cates, who was the gymnastics teacher at Frostig.

I didn't learn to ride a bike till I was 12 or 13, at which point I got too embarrassed to be the only teenager still on training wheels.

BTW, I always advise parents that if you need to teach your kid to ride a bike, don't run up and down the street holding onto the seat till you let go and your kid falls down on the concrete and suffers third degree burns on their elbows and knees.

Nope, not smart. Don't do it.

Instead, train your kid to bike-ride on a beach so if they fall it's just nice soft sand.

Speaking of beach, my cousin Beth, who competed in the Olympic trials when she was young, taught me how to swim. I'm a pretty good swimmer now: freestyle, breaststroke, even butterfly.

GOLF WARS

Every week or so, Dad and me drove over to a Putt-N-Play miniature golf course in Encino, in the Valley.

The 18-hole course had all kinds of cool stuff, a castle, rivers, walkways, doors—it was like a maze you had to struggle to get out of.

The first few times we went, Dad instructed me as I stood over the ball, golf club in hand.

"Okay, Chris, you see that little line that runs down the head of the club?"

"Uh-uh."

"Good. What you wanna do is, line up that line with the ball. That line is where you want to hit the ball."

I brought the club back to swing.

"Wait. Right before you hit the ball, your instinct will be to look where you want the ball to go. But don't. It'll mess up your swing."

"Okay. So...?"

"Line up your shot *before* you swing. Then, keep your head down and just stroke the ball."

I followed his instructions. Week by week, I improved.

In fact, I got so good at it that, after a while, Dad proposed a side-bet: $2 per hole to the winner of that hole. At the end of the game, whoever won the most holes had to treat the other person to lunch.

I was in my teens before I finally beat him and had to buy him lunch. "Okay, putz, you won, but now you're not getting any more gimmies."

You see, a gimme was like a freebie: if I hit the ball too hard and it went off the pad, he'd let me not count the stroke, just do it over. So, with no more gimmies, my new goal was to beat him straight out.

Since the most either of us ever won was ten out of the eighteen holes, the winner walked away with $20, which meant lunch at McDonald's: Big Macs, fries, and diet Cokes.

Finally, when I was 14, I sunk *three hole-in-ones*.

"Damn, Chris! I taught you too well."

PUTZ VS. SCHMUCK

Often, when my father felt particularly affectionate towards me, he'd call me a *putz*.

"Nice going, *putz*."

And whenever he said something particularly stupid, which was often, I'd say, "Nice going, *schmuck*."

The Putz *and the* schmuck.

GOLF WARS 2

Every year at the Frostig golf tournament, there was a putting contest.

The way it worked was, when the event kicked off on Friday night, there would be an auction where attendees could bid on one of the celebrity teams—two celebs per team—who would compete against each other on Saturday.

The bidder who got the winning team was rewarded with an all-expenses-paid trip to Hawaii or Europe.

One year, the celebrity who was to play with Dad had to cancel last minute. Rather than show up with *bupkes*, Dad asked me to take the celeb's place.

"No," I said. "No-no-no-no-no. Are you nuts? First of all, I'm not a celebrity."

"Are you kidding? Of course you are! You're the poster-child of Frostig, of the whole damn tournament."

"Second of all, I'm not going to compete in a putting contest in front of 500 people."

"Come on, Chris, you can do this. You're a terrific putter."

Then he delivered his oft-repeated credo: "Chris, the only time you fail in life is when you don't try. Give it a shot."

I gave it a shot.

Lo and behold, with all the years of Dad's advice and instruction at miniature golf, I scored two hole-in-ones and beat him.

Dad was ambivalent about his defeat. On the one hand, he was the proud papa.

On the other hand, my father was always very competitive and was not ever happy about losing: "Damn, my son showed me up at the golf tournament that *I started*."

HARVEY WHO?

I've been talking about my father as if the entire world knows who he was, but for those readers too young to have watched The Carol Burnett Show—which is now available on YouTube, go watch some episodes—you may remember him as the evil Blazing Saddles character, Hedley Lamar.

Who else but a classically trained Shakespearean actor could pull off Hedley's famous line, "My mind is a raging torrent, flooded with rivulets of thought, cascading into a waterfall of creative alternatives."

Young Harvey in the Navy.

NOT-SO-SMARTY-PANTS

I was eight when Dad took Maria and me to Hawaii for a vacation.

By now, I was pretty good at taking care of myself, in so far as the basic conditions of life were concerned: I knew not to run out into traffic; not to stick my hand into a hot oven; to wash hands after using the toilet; to brush teeth in the morning and before bed; and to dress nicely, because people judge you by your appearance. ("The apparel oft proclaims the man," Dad oft proclaimed.)

In Hawaii, the first morning at the hotel, I washed, brushed my teeth, and got dressed, my apparel highlighted by a clean well-pressed Hawaiian shirt.

The family went down for breakfast.

I can't remember what I ordered, but I do remember that, as we finished our meal, Dad suddenly stared at me.

"Chris," he said, "I see you have on a very nice shirt, and your tennis shoes—and socks. But guess what?"

With that, he raised my shirt and there, in front of some 200 hotel guests, I was exposed wearing, under the nice shirt, only my tighty-whiteys.

"Where are your pants?" he asked.

I shrugged. "Up in the room, I guess."

"Why didn't you put them on?"

"I guess I forgot. I was excited about breakfast."

"Aren't you embarrassed?"

"Now I am. Now that you pulled my shirt up."

"Oh. Sorry."

And he burst out laughing.

Dad's laughter was maniacal; it filled whatever room he was in. I fled the restaurant and ran up to our hotel room.

Of course, I didn't have the room key, so I just stood in the hall in my Hawaiian shirt and underpants and waited for Dad and Maria.

BESTIES

I had a really good friend at Frostig: Charles Reid.

He was a big kid with a big smile, very outgoing. And he always wore a heavy winter Miami Dolphin jacket, no matter how hot it was outside.

"Charles," I'd say, "we're in Los Angeles, it's the middle of July, it's, like, 104 degrees in the shade, take the heavy jacket off."

"I don't want people to see my fat stomach."

One day, I came home from school to find my mother grim-faced, ashen. She sat me down and explained that Charles and some other kids had been playing cowboys and Indians in his backyard and somehow Charles got entangled in a clothesline. His friends thought he was clowning around and ran off, leaving him there to hang to death.

It slowly sank in.

"Charles? He's dead?"

"Yes."

She hugged me close as I sobbed.

RULES

Growing up, the most important rule in our house was that I do my homework every day.

I got out of school at three o'clock and was home by three-thirty. Normally, I could spend the entire afternoon on my assignments, even, if necessary, finishing them after dinner.

But whenever Dad was on the Burnett show, if I wanted to watch the taping, I had to whip through my homework so I could be ready to leave with him no later than four-thirty, in order to avoid freeway traffic out to Burbank.

The same rule applied for baseball games, appearances on the Johnny Carson show, family events, anything: homework and chores came first.

Other than homework, Dad's chief bugaboo was leaving food remains in my room.

"Chris! Why is there a *banana peel* under your bed? *Again.*"

"Sorry."

"And yesterday, half a Swiss cheese sandwich on your desk. Without a plate."

That was another thing, plates: Dad was big on plates.

"Food goes on plates," he'd say, "*not* in a paper towel!"

FAREWELL

I spent ten years as the poster child for Frostig.

Dad used to joke—or maybe boast—that I knew the school so well, that when they hired a new principal, I was the one who gave her the official school tour.

The reason I was in elementary school for ten years is that they didn't have actual first grade, second grade, third grade, etc. At the end of each school year, they made an evaluation. There were certain goals that you had to meet to advance to the next level. If you didn't meet them, you were given extra help to eventually achieve the next level.

There was no graduation ceremony per se; after "grade six" you were done. I would've loved an actual ceremony, but that wasn't their thing.

It was just, "Bye-bye, Frostig."

FOOD

My father loved food. He used to say Jews are either eating, thinking about their next meal, or cooking it.

Dad enjoyed cooking; unfortunately, his repertoire was limited. Once a week he'd hit the kitchen to whip up either steak and mashed potatoes or macaroni and cheese. The rest of the week, he'd examine the contents of the refrigerator, shoot a glance at the pantry, and pronounce, "Okay, I'm bored with this, let's make reservations."

Mom, from Wisconsin, was big on cheese. Cheese and fish. She cooked the best salmon ever. And her salmon salad, mmmm!

Aside from salmon, steak and potatoes, and mac and cheese, we ate in a lot of restaurants, and indulged in lots of weird (to a kid) ethnic cuisines. Typically, the server would arrive at our table with platters and bowls of some hideous-looking, horrible-smelling goop.

Then Mom or Dad would say, "Try this, Chris."

I'd shut my eyes, open my mouth, and a fork or chopsticks would be thrust into my maw. I may have winced, made a face, or gagged, but I never vomited in a restaurant.

Yay!

CHINESE PIZZA

Dad was a pizza fanatic. By "fanatic," I mean he actually had a brick oven installed in our house.

Since he was from Chicago, he insisted that the only pizza worth eating was deep-dish style, like back home.

Oh, and Chinese food. He was pretty crazy about Chinese food. There's this whole Jewish custom of celebrating Christmas by going to the movies and eating Chinese food.

Yeah, Dad was traditional that way.

RELIGION 101

Let me clarify Dad's love for food; it was more than an obsession, it was a *religion*.

Every Sunday, Dad worshipped at the altar of Nate'n Al, a legendary Jewish deli in Beverley Hills.

He'd phone in, place his order, drive over to pick it up, and return to the house with four gigantic bags.

Out would come bagels (onion, garlic, poppy-seed), cream cheese (plain, scallion, olive), all manner of smoked fish (Nova Scotia, belly lox, sable, white fish, kippered herring), blintzes (cheese, potato), a container of sour pickles, a container of sauerkraut, and, for dessert, lemon pound-cake, his favorite.

That was our typical Sunday: the family hanging out, swimming, kibitzing—with, during baseball season, the Dodgers game on TV in the background—and taking frequent breaks to hit the enormous spread of food Dad had laid out on the dining room table.

He was also inclined to celebrate special occasions at Nate'n Al. For example, in 1986, when I was home from Landmark College for Easter vacation, I had a physical exam at the doctor's, which, coincidentally (or not?) was right down the block from Nate'n Al.

My test results showed a cholesterol level through the roof.

After receiving the doctor's admonitions, Dad took me to Nate'n Al for lunch. He ordered scrambled eggs with lox and onions, bagels with cream cheese and smoked sable, potato pancakes with sour cream and apple sauce, and, to wash it down, Dr. Brown's cream soda.

"Dad, the doctor said I'm not supposed to eat this stuff. I'm too young to die."

I was 22.

"*Putz*, cholesterol is just a number. You're young and healthy. Enjoy life. Here, have another blintz."

HERE'S JOHNNY!

One Christmas when I was eight, a package arrived for me with a card that said, "Merry Christmas from J. Carson."

I had no idea who J. Carson was. I opened the box. And inside was a black-and-gold Casio calculator. Only it was more than a calculator; it could play music and do all sorts of brainy things.

I asked Dad, "Who's J. Carson?"

"Johnny Carson."

"Why would Johnny Carson give me a Christmas present?"

"We're friends."

"Huh."

I knew Dad had been on Johnny's show but I had no idea they were that close.

The next time Dad did a *Tonight Show* spot, I came along and thanked Johnny for the gift.

He shook my hand, patted me on the back, and complimented me on my politeness.

DIVORCE

By '74, my parents were not getting along so great.

In 1977, they divorced.

Like most children in that situation—particularly children with disability issues like mine—I harbored a sense of guilt, a feeling that I was somehow the cause of their break-up.

Or, at the least, that my LD had put pressure on their marriage.

Both Mom and Dad went out of their way to assure me that, whatever problems they had were of their own doing, and definitely not my fault.

In fact, under the circumstances, they had what most people would call, particularly for a Hollywood/celebrity separation, an "amicable divorce."

Mom was friendly with another actor, George DiCenzo. After the divorce, Mom moved in with George, to his house in Malibu.

My initial concerns—would George be my new father? What would happen to my real father? — were soon allayed. George and Dad became good friends. Every Christmas, Dad came over with caviar and goodies, and George would haul out bottles of Champagne.

Dad and stepdad whipping up goodies.

In fact, George made it clear that he was my *step*father and would never attempt to supersede my father's authority.

Relaxing with George.

Sometimes I wished that Dad was not on such great terms with George because if I did something I shouldn't have in one house or the other, the consequence would be carried over.

There were ways, though, that George's parenting differed from Dad's. While both my mother and father gave me unconditional love, unconditional support, sometimes, in light of my LD, they may have been a tad too forgiving, a bit too lenient in letting me get away with things.

George had more of a tough-love attitude, like he wasn't going to buy into the poor-poor-pitiful Chris thing.

For example, growing up in my parents' home, we always had a housekeeper; although we had a washing machine and dryer, I never had to do my own laundry.

That didn't work for George. He showed me how to use the washing machine and dryer, and fold up my clothes. And take out the trash and recycling, walk the dogs, feed the cats, and help around the house when asked. He also taught me how to how to cook a few things, mostly breakfast and snack-food items. In fact, George was a gourmet chef, especially when it came to Italian food, especially pasta, though he favored it served the traditional Italian way, al dente.

Sorry, George, but if I never again eat half-cooked spaghetti, I'll die a happy camper.

RELIGION 2

After food, my father's secondary religion was baseball, and God was the Los Angeles Dodgers.

Dad, Ron Clark, who was in *High Anxiety* and *History of the World, Part I* with Dad, and Ernie Anderson, *The Love Boat*'s voice, shared four season tickets to Dodgers Stadium—out near Chavez Ravine—which meant they each could attend about a third of the Dodgers' home games.

Dad took me to all the games he went to, about 25 games a season.

It was a bonding time for us, where he pointed out the nuances of the sport. He always said you had to love baseball first and your team second; if the opposing team outplayed yours, you had to give them credit.

Dodger games allowed him an opportunity to combine his love for food and baseball. Besides the traditional hot dogs, peanuts, and Cracker Jacks, there were nachos, burgers, fries, ice cream sandwiches, you name it, all washed down with plenty of beer for him, soda for me.

SURPRISE!

We were at a Dodgers game for my eighth birthday. Dad, Maria, and McLean Stevenson, who played Lt. Colonel Henry Blake on the TV series *M*A*S*H*, and was one of Dad's best friends.

During the third inning, while the visiting team was at bat, McLean excused himself to go the men's room. It seemed like he was gone for a long time, but that's always a thing with celebrities when they're out in public, being besieged by fans who ask for autographs, so I didn't pay much attention to his lengthy absence.

But then, after the fifth inning, a sign flashed up on the huge scoreboard: HAPPY BIRTHDAY, CHRIS KORMAN! NUMBER 8!

I was shocked, dumbstruck.

"Dad, how do they know it's my birthday? How do they even know I'm here?"

Dad answered with an elaborate shrug. When I turned to McLean, he winked.

Of course, he'd gone to the announcer's booth and set it up.

P.S.: After a dozen or so seasons of rooting for mediocre Dodger teams, Dad made a difficult decision:

"I'm not going to drive all the way out to Chavez Ravine to watch the Dodgers choke again."

LESSONS FROM DAD

A typical math or English test at Frostig involved the teacher holding a stopwatch and telling us, "You have ten minutes to answer these twenty questions."

I normally didn't test well; I was nervous before and during the test and later, when I saw the grade, became seriously bummed out.

Frustrated, and depressed.

One day, after a miserable grade, Dad sat me down and said, "Chris, I think you're missing the point. What they're really looking for is your accuracy and penmanship. So don't worry about how many answers you can come up with in ten minutes. Just take the questions one at a time, do as many as you can correctly. And make sure your penmanship is neat."

I also let him know that I wasn't good at art.

"Putz, art isn't something you have to be good at. The whole point is to have fun. You use crayons in class?"

"Yeah."

"Okay, so draw something you like. A golf club. A tree. A self-portrait."

"Maybe I could draw, like, that castle at the Pitch-N-Putt. With the river that goes around it. The moat."

"The moat. Good word!"

It suddenly became clear to me that, for him, the effort I put into learning a subject, whether in multiplication or division or English, science, or art, the effort was more important than the grade.

JAWS

When I was 13, I needed an operation on my jaw to correct an under-bite. Medically, the procedure was called *orthognathic surgery*.

The prospect scared the hell out of me. Even the words orthognathic surgery were frightening.

Dad must have mentioned my fear to Carol because she invited us out to dinner, where she explained that she had had similar surgery, only for her it was the opposite, an over-bite.

She told me she, too, had been deathly afraid of going under the knife. She told me about her post-surgery routine, which sounded pretty ghastly, though between Dad and Carol egging each other on, I did manage a few laughs.

For the osteotomy, as it was called, the surgeon would cut a piece of jawbone away, then tie the teeth together to let the jaw heal. Which meant I would not be able to eat solid foods for two or three months.

"Be sure to get a turkey baster," Carol told Dad.

The thought of taking all my meals through a turkey baster cracked me up.

Sure enough, after the procedure, I could only drink liquids, no solid food, nothing you'd have to chew. Just stuff you could liquefy in a blender and sip through a straw.

Before the surgery I weighed 118 pounds, and because I drank at least six milkshakes a day my weight ballooned.

Besides the milkshakes, Mom made me protein shakes and drinks with green stuff.

Colgate between my lips, sip some water through a straw, slosh the toothpaste around, and then somehow spit it all out the side of my mouth.

More often than not I wound up swallowing a mouthful of toothpaste liquid.

Yum.

MINDING DAD

Prior to the start of the 1981 TV season (yes, there were "seasons" back then) NBC held a huge event for the shows it was going to debut. One of them was an offshoot of the Burnett show called *Mama's Family*. The show starred Carol, Vicki Lawrence, Betty White, and my father.

I was Dad's date for the event.

Since he would be introduced on stage, he wore a tuxedo. But since we would be rushing out to a Dodgers game right after the minimum amount of time NBC compelled their stars to attend—one hour—he also wore his Dodgers baseball cap.

The reason he took me to this thing was because he had no idea who any of the NBC television stars were, and I could quickly fill him in.

Movies he knew. Cary Grant, yes; Burt Lancaster, yes; Bette Davis, Jerry Lewis, Gary Cooper, yes-yes-yes.

So my function was to stick close to his side and quickly answer the evening's ongoing whispered question: "Chris, who's that?"

And I'd whisper back, "Ed Begley Jr. From *St. Elsewhere*."

One of the new shows was *Remington Steele*, a detective series starring Pierce Brosnan, who would go on to play James Bond in film. But not yet. Now he was "only" a budding television star.

"Dad," I whispered, Pierce Brosnan is coming at you."

"Who?"

I turned towards him and rapid-fired: "Pierce-Brosnan-Remington-Steele-don't-say-anything-stupid."

I lost that one.

Pierce introduced himself and stuck out his hand to shake. "Hi, I'm Pierce Brosnan, from *Remington Steele*."

"Oh, right," said my father as he shook Pierce's hand, "you're that guy on Stephanie Zimbalist's show."

Pierce froze.

He and Dad eyeballed each other. Me, I looked for an escape hatch.

After an eternity, Dad broke into a huge grin. "Come on, Pierce, I was kidding, of course I knew you were the star of the show."

"Oh. Ha. Funny. Well, great to meet you." And he headed off.

My father stood there and gazed after him.

Finally, he turned to me and said, "Well, wha'd'ya know, Remington Steele can't take a joke."

"Schmuck. And I can't take you anywhere."

"Lighten up, *putz*. Come on, let's grab some food and then get the hell out of here."

Go, Dodgers!

MEL

A History of the World Part 1, directed by Mel Brooks and starring him and my father, was partially shot in Shepperton Studios, in London.

During a school break, Dad flew Maria and me over.

On the set, there were director's chairs; each chair had the name of a star or the director stenciled on the back.

When I arrived, Mel got up from his chair and said, "Chris, here, sit in my chair."

"Oh, wow, thanks."

"Hungry? Let me get you something. You want a bagel? A knish? A banger?"

"What's a banger?"

"It's like an English hotdog."

"Thanks, but no, I should be getting you something to eat."

"I'm fine. Sit."

Many years later, Mel wrote the musical adaptation of his classic film *The Producers*. After it opened, Dad went to see it. Apparently, he mentioned to someone that the Matthew Broderick-Nathan Lane coupling wasn't as good as the film's original Zero Mostel-Gene Wilder pairing.

News of Dad's opinion got back to Mel.

After Dad died, Mel was there for the funeral and spoke adoringly of him.

Later, he took me aside.

"Chris, if you ever need a favor, just call me. I loved your father, even though he could be a real asshole."

MY LESS-THAN-FAVORITE YEAR

One evening in 1982, Dad, Maria, and I were having dinner at Spago's when I spotted Mark Linn-Baker, with a drink and cigarette.

Mark had recently co-starred with Peter O'Toole in *My Favorite Year*.

"Dad," I whispered, "there's Mark Linn-Baker over there."

"Wow. You know, My Favorite Year was his very first movie."

"Yes, I know. Why don't you go over and say hi?"

Dad considered that for a second or two, then said, "Chris, do me a favor, go ask him for a cigarette."

"I'm fourteen. I don't smoke."

"But I do."

"Then you go ask him for a cigarette."

Dad gave me the evil eye. "Don't be a putz."

I got up and walked over to the new star.

"Hello, Mr. Baker. Sorry to disturb you, but I wonder if I could please bum a cigarette."

"You smoke?"

"No, but my father does."

"Then why doesn't he ask me?"

"He didn't want to bother you."

Mark smiled. "So he sent you to bother me."

"He also doesn't like to be recognized."

"Oh? Who's your father?"

"Harvey Korman."

He just about fell out of his chair. *"Your father is Harvey Korman?"*

"Yeah."

"Let's go."

He stood and grabbed his pack of cigarettes, and I escorted him back to our table.

"Harvey, it's so great to meet you!"

"My pleasure. I loved your work in *My Favorite Year*."

"Thank you. I love *all* your work."

"We're about to order dessert, please join us." Mark joined us.

We ordered cheesecake.

Mark and Dad drank coffee, smoked cigarettes, and regaled each other with compliments.

Maria and I sat there, ate our cheesecake, and pretended not to be bored.

Maria and me.

FATHER KNOWS BEST

When I was young, Dad fought for me at every step of the way, but he also demanded that I need to become my own advocate.

"Chris, nobody's going to care about your rights as much as you. You need to learn what your rights are, what your strengths and weaknesses are, and be able to articulate them. I'm not gonna be around forever, *you* have to be your own business card, your own billboard, your own brand."

SPEAK THE SPEECH I PRAY YOU

From 1981 to 1983, I attended Clearview Junior High School, which is now known as Westview.

Westview is a supportive, structured educational program for students in grades 6 through 12 with learning differences, ADHD, high-functioning ASD, and/or mild emotional problems.

https://www.thehelpgroup.org/school/westview/

I took speech pathology with Michael Desaro who, outside of my father, was a major influence in my life; a godsend.

Michael had me do tongue twisters like "She sells seashells on the sea shore" to get me to speak clearer.

I'd recite them into a tape recorder, listen to them, and re-record them, over and over, striving for clarity and speed.

My next developmental leap—fasten your seat-belts, folks—was to step out on stage and perform.

To act in a play.

Eek!

Oh sure, I'd been "performing" at Frostig golf tournaments since I was five, and yes, my father was one of the most talented, most respected actors in the business, but the thing is, if you're playing a role you have to be able to comprehend and remember your lines and then recite them with understanding and clarity; exactly those qualities which I lacked.

Nevertheless, the teachers at Clearview persuaded me to play an important role in their production of *Bye Bye Birdie*, that of Harry McAfee, who was famously played in the film version by the great comedic actor Paul Lynde.

BYE BYE BIRDIE

I never auditioned for lead roles. Hey, I'm the son of a second banana and the son of a second banana doesn't fall far from the banana tree. (Though, technically, bananas grow on plants, not on trees.)

I wasn't interested in an acting career. Theater, for me, was fun, a chance to hang out with cool people, and an opportunity to play a character, to get out of myself, to pretend to be somebody else.

Of course, with my learning disability, memorizing lines was a real problem, a huge problem.

Dad came up with a solution. I would study three pages of dialogue, and recite them, to the best of my memory, into a tape recorder. Then I'd play it back and note where I was off or what I was missing. Back to the script for another round of study, and another round of taping.

In that way, I got through nine pages a day, sixty pages a week without hardly realizing it.

Sixty pages because I was actually playing two characters: Mr. McAfee and Sam, the Mayor.

As Mr. McAfee, I had a song, "What's the Matter with Kids Today?"

Dad's advice: "Don't imitate Paul Lynde. Try to find the essence of the character. Break the song down into individual phrases and work on those phrases one at a time."

He spent a whole week helping me on phrasing and timing.

I got to attend the Harvard of Comedy, right in my own living room.

THE 6.5-SECOND RULE

If I needed a good example of how to not try to imitate Paul Lynde, my father provided it via his portrayal of Rhett Butler—Rhatt Butler, they called him—on The Carol Burnett Show. He definitely did not try to channel Clark Gable. No, Dad was a Harvey Korman/Jewish Southern-gentleman.

A big part of his talent lay in his mastery of comedic timing.

"Chris, when you memorize a script, you know where a line should get a laugh, right?"

"Yeah."

"But when you're performing, sometimes the audience may surprise you with a laugh you totally didn't expect."

"So…"

"Well, the problem is, if you get a surprise laugh, it can produce a kind of adrenaline rush, and then your natural inclination will be to deliver your next line right away, right over the laugh."

"Tim does that."

"Right, and I tell him all the time, I yell at him. 'Tim! When you get a laugh, say your name out loud and if you can't hear it, wait-wait-wait!'"

"Six-and-a-half seconds."

"What?"

"It's what you do. When you get a big laugh, you wait six-point-five seconds before your next line."

"You're kidding."

"No. Like on the *Eunice* show."

(*Eunice* was a 90-minute TV pilot, an offshoot of the "Mama's Family" shtick from the Burnett show.)

"What did I do on the *Eunice* show?"

"There's this episode where you hugged Eunice and said, 'I want you to come over to my house, I got a new phonograph needle.' Huge laugh."

"Oh yeah, that was a surprise."

"Six-and-a-half seconds."

"Chrissy, don't you have anything better to do with your day?"

"No. I have nothing better to do with my day than study you perform. The way you actually listen to the other actors."

"Thank you. That's very sweet. But, you know, it's all about the writing. And you know what the difference is between a great writer whose words can actually be heard by the audience, and a great writer where the actors talk over a laugh-line?"

"Uh…"

"The writer whose words are heard loud and clear gets to eat at Spago's. The other writer, at McDonald's."

THE ONE-HIT WONDER

Bye Bye Birdie went over so well that I was emboldened to write and perform a skit in the school's annual Christmas Show, a satire of *Saturday Night Live.*

Yeah, a satire of a satire.

My skit was set in a Christmas-tree lot. A *gay* Christmas tree lot. Yes, and I played a homosexual Christmas tree. During our dress rehearsal, I was seized with the sense that the piece was awful, dreadful, humiliating, and my performance just a total embarrassment.

It was the only time I wished my father didn't come to see me perform, but not only did he attend, he also brought along his old pal Dick van Patten, whom I'd known my entire life.

And to make matters worse, they sat in the very front row, stage left, from where I made my entrance. They were the first thing I saw when I walked out on stage, costumed as a gay Christmas tree.

The sight of them sitting there drove me right out of character, my opening line replaced with the thought, *If this doesn't drive me into psychosis I don't know what will.*

RISING STAR

After that gay-Christmas-tree disaster, I went on to do several other plays. It was tons of fun to get up on stage wearing costumes, pretending to be characters who weren't me, and working with other kids who had various LDs.

My drama teacher said, "I don't need to bother with you, Chris, with what you have at home."

Yep, being Harvey Korman's son meant I had one of the best acting instructors in the world at my beck-and-call 24/7.

But it was also a double-edged sword, because if you're Harvey Korman's son, everyone expects you to be brilliant; there was a lot of pressure, though mostly outweighed by the excitement, fun, and attention.

Was there any parental concern that, with all the positive feedback, I'd decide to become a real actor, with an agent and manager? That I'd start the never-ending process of auditions?— a process Mom and Dad were well familiar with from suffering through his early years of rejection-rejection-rejection: the tension-filled days waiting to hear back from a casting director; the crushed hopes when you find out that the role of a lifetime, that you knew you were perfect for, was awarded to a lesser talent; the miserable day jobs you were forced to endure in order to pay the rent and put food on the table.

Although they did not directly express concerns about a possible future for me as an actor, I would've well understood their anxiety.

You see, despite Dad's success and acclaim, he felt frustrated and unfulfilled with the acting profession.

He was classically trained. He'd studied acting and improv at the Goodman Theatre in Chicago, then technique and scene study at the Herbert Berghof Studio in New York with Tony Award-winner Uta Hagen.

Miss Hagen, as she insisted her students call her, taught such brilliant actors as Geraldine Paige, Hal Holbrook, and Charles Nelson Reilly, to name a few, but declared that her best students were Matthew Broderick, David Hyde-Pierce, and my father.

In 1955, Dad performed in a production of *Hamlet* at the Guild Theatre in Santa Monica. Afterwards, both Charles Laughton and Bette Davis came backstage to congratulate him. They later told a reporter that Dad was going to be the next Laurence Olivier, the finest stage and screen actor of his time.

But Broadway did not open its arms.

Dad would say, "The producers, the critics, the audience, they all wanted a young, good-looking Adonis. All I could offer them was an aging, balding Jew."

Dad could sing, he could dance, he could act, but back in the '60s, at the start of his career, there were only three TV channels—CBS, ABC, and NBC—and once they pigeon-holed you, that kind of determined your career.

Dad became Carol's second banana.

WHAT'S A SECOND BANANA?

One of Dad's baseball pals once explained to me the second banana concept.

"He's the butter-and-eggs man. He manages to get on base, which allows the top banana, the hitter, to deliver the clean-up shot."

In other words, the second banana sets up the joke, so the top banana can pop the punchline and get the laugh.

Think Dean Martin for Jerry Lewis; Bud Abbot for Lou Costello; my father for Carol Burnett.

Although Dad came to resent the classification, he took his comedic work very seriously. Before each Carol Burnett show, he was petrified. He was the family breadwinner; if he screwed up, he'd be out of a job, would be unable to support us, unable to put food on the table.

But after ten years of live TV, he felt totally burnt out doing a weekly show; he turned down *The Love Boat*'s lead role of Captain Stubing.

Admiration for his ten years of cross-dressing came from such "serious" actors as Burt Lancaster, Gary Cooper, and Cary Grant, each of whom, when their paths crossed, went out of their way to admire his acting skill.

It was small consolation for a classically-trained second-banana.

SNATCH

I was seven years old when *Blazing Saddles* came out. My parents refused to allow me to see it because of "that kind of language."

I argued with Dad, "Any time I wanna hear *that kind of language*, I'll spend an hour hanging out with Buddy."

Buddy Hackett was one of my father's best friends and a famous foul-mouthed comedian.

Dad relented.

For me, age seven, the funniest stuff in the movie were the sight-gags, like when Mongo punches the horse and it falls down.

But there were verbal bits that everyone in the theater cracked up laughing about, that I just didn't get. For example, when Dad's character, Hedley Lamarr, tries to figure out how to do a "land snatch," and he consults a dictionary, and is referred to "snatch."

The Blazing Saddles *Era.*

THE PADDLE SCENE

On Dad's first day on the *Blazing Saddles* set, his first scene was with Mel Brooks and Robyn Hilton. Dad had to say all his lines while hitting a paddle ball.

Years later, he confessed how pressured he felt to be in the same scene with the brilliant writer/director of the film, right off the bat.

"Plus, I had to keep that damn paddle ball going without hitting Mel in the head or Robyn in the boobs."

After Dad died, Mel came over to me at the memorial and told me that he was never worried about getting bopped on the bean, and that he and my father had an immediate chemistry.

"Whatever scene your father was in, he elevated every actor in that scene."

THE DESERT LIFE

The beans/belching/farting scene in *Blazing Saddles* was shot in the Arizona desert.

Slim Pickens, to get into character, stayed overnight in his camper with his Winchester rifle and his dog.

Dad was delighted that he didn't have to be in that scene; he didn't like to travel and the thought of traipsing way the hell across the desert was a horrible proposition.

Years later, when a friend of his asked why his son (me) had moved to Las Vegas—in the Mojave Desert—he replied, "Don't most Jews end up in the desert?"

QUIZ SHOW

Whenever we drove anywhere, which in LA is *everywhere*, Dad liked to play quiz-games with me.

When I was young, I had to memorize every state in the union, in alphabetical order. Then, the state capitals.

Moving on from there, we played the Initials Game, with a focus on baseball and actors, two subjects we both knew a lot about.

For example, he might say, "JM."

And I'd reply, "Juan Marichal," a right-handed Hall of Fame pitcher for the Giants.

"Too easy, Chris. Uh, let's see. Okay, CL."

"Cookie Lavagetto."

"Damn. Okay, got another one. GG."

Switching to actors. Sneaky.

"Greta Garbo."

"TC."

"Tony Curtis."

"KD."

"Kirk Douglas."

"Enough! Is that all you know about, baseball and celebrities?"

"The nut doesn't fall far from the tree."

OMG! It's Harvey Korman's Son!

Like father, like son.

IT'S HEDLEY!

Driving in Los Angeles can be hellish.

Whenever Dad and I were stuck in traffic, we'd pass the time—long after I'd outgrown naming all the states in alphabetic order, then their capitals, then guessing the names of baseball players and actors by their initials—we'd run lines from movies Dad had been in. One of us would spout a line, and the other one would have to respond with the response.

So, say we'd be coming from a McDonald's on our way to Dodger Stadium. Dad would have gobbled up his Big Mac and fries in two minutes, while I still had my meal on my lap.

He'd say, "Look, Herman, I'm in Hedy Lamarr's shoes."

"'*Hedley.*' Too easy, Dad. Try this one: 'My mind is a raging torrent, flooded with rivulets of thought cascading into a waterfall of creative alternatives.'"

"'Ditto.'"

"No. 'Ditto' goes after 'My mind is aglow with whirling, transient nodes of thought careening through a cosmic vapor of invention.'"

"Oh, right. Okay, give me the other line again."

"'My mind is a raging torrent, flooded with rivulets of thought cascading into a waterfall of creative alternatives.'"

"'God darnit Mr. Lamarr, you use your tongue prettier than a twenty-dollar whore.'"

"Perfect."

To reward himself, Dad snatched one of my French fries.

"Hey, you already ate yours!"

"It's good to be the king."

"Whoa. We were doing *Blazing Saddles*, not *History of the World Part I*."

"Like I said—"

"—And that wasn't even your line, that was Mel's line. You weren't even in the scene."

"Like I said, *putz*, 'It's good to be the king.'"

FANDOM

My father was a very private person, almost to the point of shyness. When he wasn't doing a film or TV show, he'd adopt various disguises to prevent public recognition.

One time at Magic Mountain, as we came off a ride, Dad, in a mustache and beard, with huge sunglasses and a Dodgers baseball cap, was immediately mobbed by fans asking for autographs.

He was gracious about it.

Later, when I asked him how those people recognized him in his clever disguise, he said, "It's my nose, I have a very distinctive honker."

"But can't you just ignore them, just walk away?" "Chris, you don't bite the hand that feeds you."

BESTIES 2

I attended Landmark High School from 1983 - 1985.

My best friend there was Scott Marshall. We did everything together.

Scott had cerebral palsy and was confined to a wheelchair. Compared to him, how could I possibly complain about my learning disability?

One year, over Easter break, we went to Disneyland.

During any school vacation, Disneyland becomes a nightmare: as you can imagine, the most famous theme park in the world is packed to the rafters with overexcited kids and their over-stressed parents. The lines for rides stretch for miles, with signs like "You are only one hour away from Space Mountain."

"Damn," I said, "an hour wait."

"Don't be silly, Chris, we're not gonna wait on line for *any* rides. Come on."

I pushed his chair right to the front. Nobody on line said a word, and the Disney ride attendants waved us right in.

How cool!

But after the ride, I turned totally hypocritical.

"Scott, you exploited your handicap!"

"Chris, you milk it where you can milk it."

PARANOIA STRIKES DEEP

By now, my dad's reluctance to be recognized in public morphed into a downright fear of being stalked.

He was so terrified about strangers knowing where he lived that he didn't even want my friends to know the address. If I was going out, he'd make sure I had change in my pocket for a telephone call.

Let's say I went to a movie with Brian Harris, a high school friend who already had a driver's license and was the only one of my friends who Dad trusted enough to know our address and drive me home.

But if we were out with other people, Brian had to drop me off near a phone booth.

I'd call home.

"Dad, I'm in Westwood." And give him the location. Twenty minutes later, he'd arrive in his little red Honda.

It was quite a sight, Dad, at six-foot-three, tooling around LA hunched down in that tiny thing.

His rationale was that when he had to stop for a red light, no one—pedestrians, other drivers, police patrol cars—no one would think that the famous Harvey Korman was at the wheel of a miniscule decrepit Honda.

Eventually the thing ascended to Honda Heaven and was mercifully replaced by a comfy Lexus.

MIND EXPANDING

Actually, my father *did* want me to know about more than baseball and the entertainment industry. There was a whole world of music, art, politics, and philosophy that he felt I should be exposed to: the more I could broaden my mind, the more I'd open up to new people and experiences.

Dad himself was self-taught, an autodidact. (A word he made me learn and use in a sentence.)

He did a lot of crossword puzzles and urged me to do them as well. I tried, but...

"Dad, why the hell do I need to know an Italian word for *shoe*?"

POST-TOURNEY DEPRESSION

After every golf tournament, Dad drove us back from Palm Springs to Mom and George's house in Santa Monica. A two-hour trip.

I remember one drive in particular. It was 1985, I was enrolled in Landmark.

As soon as we hit the road, we spoke about the tournament, the highs and lows, which celebrities had been fun, which ones not-so-much.

Then we talked about baseball, about movies past and present, about life. After a while, I got quiet.

"What's up, Chris?"

"I don't know, it's just... every time, after a tournament, I feel..."

"A letdown?"

"Yeah. For three days I'm on a pedestal. Everyone is super-nice. 'Hey, you're Harvey Korman's son!' Then I go back to school and, all of a sudden, I'm nobody. I mean, I'm just Chris Korman again. It feels weird. Sometimes I resent it, that after three days of being in the spotlight... all of a sudden it's gone."

"I understand exactly how you feel. It's the same with me. When I work, I'm in the spotlight, on stage, on TV, in a movie. When I'm out in public and, if I get recognized, people expect me to be *Harvey Korman*! Then, when I get home, I'm just a father, a husband, a sports fan. Joe Shmoe."

We were quiet for a while.

Then Dad said, "Maybe you should be in therapy."

"Yeah, maybe."

REALITY

After Dad dropped me off, he hung out and chatted with Mom for a while. They were on good terms.

Me, I just gave her a hug and went up to my room. I lay down on my bed and stared up at the ceiling.

I thought about the weekend. Being on stage in my tuxedo. Hobnobbing with movie stars. *Treated* like a movie star.

Tomorrow I'd be just another high school kid. And not even a normal high school kid, but one who struggled with a speech impediment and a learning disorder.

Reality kicked in.

Crash!

CHRIS GETS SHRUNK

Eventually, I did see a psychiatrist. It was in 1988 during a semester break at Colorado Mountain College.

Her office was in Colorado, which meant she probably had a lot of patients who were either celebrities or the children of celebrities. It was a good match.

She wondered why my parents pushed me to get up on stage at that first Korman Golf Tournament.

"They didn't *push* me, my father *asked* if I wanted to and I said yes."

"You were five years old. Did you know what you were letting yourself in for?"

"Uh... not exactly. I thought it would be fun."

"But you were nervous."

"Terrified."

"Of course. Your father could have just let you sit on stage with him and not make a speech."

"The thing is...I enjoyed it."

"The attention."

"Right. And every year I hosted or co-hosted the tournament, I got better at it."

"But the next day, you're depressed."

"The next few days, yeah."

"So, it's a question of balance? Weighing your need for public attention versus your post-event depression."

"Yes."

"How bad do you crave attention?"

"Probably not as much as my father. But, yeah, I like it."

"And how severe is the depression?"

"I'm not suicidal. Just...withdrawn. And, like, everything seems a little... *off*."

"It sounds to me like the attention outweighs the depression."

"Yeah. Definitely."

GIBBY AND CO. WINS IT ALL IN '88

I was also in therapy in 1988, when I was at Colorado Mountain College. 1988 is an easy year for me to remember: it's the last time the Dodgers won the World Series.

THE WEIGHT

I also saw a psychiatrist when I was at Threshold and again when I lived in Doylestown. At some point, all that therapy started to merge together. It was all about identity and self-worth.

I grew up in show business and I often feel I haven't escaped it. Right now, I'm in the area of broadcast media. As a free-lancer, I do this-and-that; generally, I try to help people find their niche—or an agent.

As much as I like to help, sometimes I feel taken advantage of. I have a wife and child to support, and people often expect me to freely give of my time and expertise.

Trish tells me, "If you think someone is using you, back out."

"Uh... Okay, I guess."

"But you enjoy it."

"Yeah."

"Don't tell people you're Harvey Korman's son. That will separate the users, who only want to bask in his aura, from the people who genuinely like you for yourself, because you're Chris Korman."

That's what I enjoyed about working at Sea World, that no one knew me as Harvey's son. I simply showed up for my shifts, worked six or eight hours, and went home.

Just like a Normal Person.

I'm active on social media, and sometimes I experience a burst of resentment that I'm Harvey Korman's son. Let's say I express an opinion. Then my post may be inundated with comments asking if that's the way I truly feel or am I channeling my father?

I've spoken with the children of other celebrities and they feel pretty much the same. There's this weight we carry, a weight formed by people's assumptions of who we are based on the public personae of our parents.

In some ways, it's been easier since Dad died. Strangers, when we're introduced, don't automatically think: *Harvey Korman's Son!*

On the other hand, Dad was always understanding about this issue; I could talk to him and feel better.

Sometimes I think Mom was right when she took a skeptical attitude about my speaking role, age five, at Dad's first Frostig Golf Tournament.

Who knows? Maybe that first exposure to an audience gave me the impetus to seek more public attention?

Or would I have walked the same road, just begun that walk at some point later in life?

Or as Yogi Berra once said, "When you come to a fork in the road, take it."

SESAME STREET PIMP

My father was not known for being a fashion plate. His clothing closet was acquired by ravaging the wardrobe department of the Burnett show during their annual clear-the-warehouse sale.

One time I said to him, "Dad, you look like a pimp on Sesame Street."

He thought about that for a minute, then asked, "They have pimps on Sesame Street?"

HOLLYWOOD SQUARES

I wasn't a big *Hollywood Squares* fan, even though my father was often on it, but the show was recorded in the same NBC Burbank facility as the news and the NBC soap operas *Santa Barbara* and *Days of our Lives*.

I was a huge *Days* fan, so any time Dad was on *Hollywood Squares*, I tagged along and roamed the long wide hallways that connected the different studios.

Sadly, I never ran into any of the *Days* stars, but I often saw Kevin Tighe, who played one of the firemen on *Emergency!* and was in the NBC studio for *Hollywood Squares*.

I didn't know that it was not okay to interact with these people so, after I said hello to Kevin and introduced myself, every time I saw him, he'd greet me with "Hey Chris, how's it going?"

Then he'd sit me down and ask about my life, like "How's school?" and "What else you been up to?"

What was really cool was that he didn't know I was "Harvey's kid"; in fact, he never asked why I was periodically roaming the NBC hallways. Nor did he call Security to kick me out.

Eventually, Kevin did run into me with Dad, made the connection, and said, "Your son is a very charming, wonderful young man."

Dad thanked him, but after the brief conversation, we walked away and, of course, he berated me. "Chris, how many times do I have to tell you, don't bother these people."

"Which people?"

"Actors. *Real* actors. Go annoy some soap opera stars, they love that."

PETER MARSHALL

My father and Peter Marshall, longtime host of *Hollywood Squares*, were best friends.

As a result of their friendship—and my peripatetic NBC Studio hangouts—I got to know and like Peter on a personal level.

When I was six or seven, he went into the hospital for some sort of surgery. One morning while he was still there in recovery, Dad said, "Okay, Chris, today we have time for one of two things. Either breakfast at IHOP, or a visit to Peter in the hospital.

"Peter."

Peter still tells the story: "Chris loves me so much that he chose to visit me in the hospital over a terrific breakfast at IHOP."

CHEATERS

In the mid-70s, CBS ran a quiz-type game show called *Tattletales*, hosted by Bert Convy.

The set-up was this: Three couples competed against each other. One member of each couple was hidden while the other member had to answer questions about the relationship. Then the positions were switched and the other partner was asked the same questions. The fun lay in how well or poorly the answers matched, how well or poorly the couple knew each other.

For every answer that matched, the couple won $100.

The couple didn't have to be an actual husband-and-wife pair or even a boyfriend-girlfriend item; my father and McLean were a team every day for a whole week.

I was backstage for the tapings.

Before their next-to-last appearance, I took McLean and Dad aside and said, "I don't get it. You guys are best friends, you've known each other for, like, thirty years, but you lost every single round."

I let that sink in and then whispered, "Don't you wanna win one?"

"Yes," Dad quickly replied.

He could be very competitive.

"Okay, when it's your turn to answer, look over at me. This—" (a tug on the ear) "—means yes, this—" (a nose scratch) "—means no."

Dad's face lit up with a very Hedley Lamar eye-twinkle. McLean just looked at me like I was an idiot.

"Chris," he said, "it's a freaking game show. Who cares who wins?" Then he noticed the expression on Dad's face.

"Harvey, what if we get caught? You really want that on your resume?"

Dad reconsidered, then turned to me. "Thanks for your help, Chris, but tomorrow I'm gonna leave you at home with the dog."

THE DISNEY VIDEO

One sunny morning in 1983, when I was 15, I came downstairs in my bathing suit and flip-flops, a towel draped over my shoulders, ready to hit the pool for a swim.

Lo and behold, in the living room were the trappings of a video shoot: lights, reflectors, TV cameras, audio equipment, the works.

I figured it was a project Dad was working on, nothing to do with me, and proceeded jaunty-jolly on my way to the pool. I was just about to dive in when Dad came running out.

"Chris, wait-wait-wait."

"What?"

"We're setting up a video shoot for the Disney channel."

"Great. Have fun."

"It's called 'Through the Mind's Eye.'"

"Uh-huh."

"You're going to do a little speaking thing."

"What? No, you do a little speaking thing, I'm gonna do a little swimming thing."

"Chris, please. It's about growing up with a learning disability."

I paused.

Dad continued: "Kids with a learning disability need to hear about your strategies for dealing with life. Their parents need to understand that with an LD you can compensate, you can endure, you can persevere, you can succeed."

His little speech got to me.

I went up to my bedroom and got dressed. Baby-blue button-front shirt, striped tie, dark-blue slacks. My shoes were nicely polished, though I didn't think they would be seen on the video.

I came back downstairs and let HAMU (hair and make-up) try to make me look air-worthy: to neaten my unruly mop of hair and cover my acne.

Dad handed me a glass of water.

I sat back and faced the interviewer.

The lights went on, the tape rolled, and I answered questions.

Years later, this video would come back to haunt me. As they say, "No good deed shall go unpunished."

CHRIS GOES TO CAMP

In June, 1983, Mom, George and me flew from Los Angeles to Boston. We spent a couple of days exploring the city where, for some strange reason, I immediately felt at home, like I'd lived there in a prior life or something.

We rented a car and drove 31.6 miles north-east to Prides Crossing, a neighborhood in Beverly, Massachusetts, where I would spend the next two months at the Landmark Summer Camp.

I loved the camp. It was exactly as promised in the brochure, which is what you see on the website now. https://www.landmarkschool.org/summer

More Than Camp
Landmark's Summer Programs serve students with dyslexia and other language-based learning disabilities (LBLD)... Students who attend our summer program... say that the program helped them gain the skills and confidence to succeed inside and outside of the classroom.

I was already a decent tennis player; that summer, I sparkled and shone on the court, and even helped some of the newbies with their serve and backhand.

Swimming? Yep, definitely improved my stroke.

Rowing a boat came naturally, though with my limited hand-eye skills, trying to navigate a canoe was always risky, with a 50-50 chance of ending up in the lake.

CHRIS LEARNS TO SKI (NOT)

Since Landmark High School was so terrific, and Landmark summer camp such a blast, my parents enrolled me in Landmark College for the fall semester, 1985.

I soon found out that the college wasn't anywhere near Boston, but way the hell up in Bumfuck, Vermont.

Sorry, I meant to say *Putney*, Vermont. Vermont? Really?

A kid from Southern California who'd only seen snow on TV or in the movies?

Vermont, where schools are typically closed on Fridays in the winter so that students and teachers can spend weekends swooshing down the slopes?

And where "winter" runs from September—first snowfall—through May, when all that snow turns to a river of slush and mud?

Yeah, *that* Vermont.

Somebody with gross motor skills sent to live in Vermont is like a death sentence. Like, "Here's a loaded gun, Chris. Point it at your temple—uh, no, the other end; yeah, that's it—and pull the trigger."

In preparation for my first day at school, Mom and George accompanied me on the trip to Putney. We stayed in Putney's sole hotel, and toured the entire town, which took all of thirty seconds.

There was a general store. And a diner.

There was a saloon. And a church.

I fumed all the way back to the hotel. Then, as the reality of my situation sank in—that on Sunday evening, Mom and George would return to California and I would be in Putnam, Vermont, totally on my own for the first time ever, all alone to deal with brand new people and a brand new situation—I totally lost it, a full-on panic attack.

"I can't do this!" I screamed.

I was met with a complete lack of sympathy.

I threw myself on a couch and buried my face in a pillow. Bits of adult conversation reached my ears.

"Maybe this was a mistake." "Maybe…"

"Maybe we should transfer him someplace closer to home."

"Maybe. Or maybe he needs to give it a chance. He's been in the Landmark system for—"

I exploded "—Yes, I've been in the Landmark system, but this is in the middle of *fucking nowhere!*"

Ultimately, the tough-love approach won out.

"Don't worry, Chris, you'll be fine."

CHRIS LEARNS TO SKI, PART 2

I wasn't fine.

It was a tough year. I was 17 years old, a kid from sunny Southern California, who knew Dodgers baseball, miniature golf, hanging out with celebrities, and trying to deal with a learning disability.

Aside from trudging through snowdrifts up to my chin, slip-sliding on ice, and avoiding countless skiing invitations, Landmark College had no idea how to deal with my needs.

Back story: Unbeknownst to my family and me, sometime in the '80s, Landmark College, for whatever reasons—perhaps to smooth their funding operation—decided to combine various disabilities into one category.

Ergo, they put dyslexia and an LD into the same group. That's like putting autism and blind people in the same category. *It's not the same!*

I didn't have dyslexia: I don't read backwards; never have, never will. The bad news: I was bored. Bored to distraction.

The good news is, my friend and classmate, Jason Adlestein, was also averse to snow.

And he had a car.

So when we got snowed in, which was almost the entire school year, and every other student headed for the snow trails, Jason and I headed for Toby's Tavern, where we ate too many Philly cheese-steak sandwiches, played too many hours of foosball, and drank way too many pitchers of beer.

L'Chaim!

CHRIS LEARNS TO SKI, PART 3

Dad was not amused.

When he arrived for parents weekend and met with some of my teachers, who informed him that I spent way too much time at Toby's Tavern and not enough time on my homework, well, no amount of complaining and explaining—how miserable I was, how Landmark was failing in their mission—nothing could persuade him that I just wasn't trying hard enough.

Up and down the length of the dorm, I could hear parents screaming at their kids about grades, about fucking up, about the cost of college, all of it.

Dad kept his cool.

"Chris, listen to me. We do our homework first, beer second. Got it?"

"So you're advocating for beer?"

"*Putz*. Don't be a smartass!"

THE DH SPEECH

For one of my classes, I had to make a presentation. It meant getting up in front of the entire class to talk about a specific topic.

Although at the Frostig golf tournaments I'd become comfortable addressing a crowd, I'd never done a presentation before.

I decided to offer up my take on the Designated Hitter.

For those who only know the rudiments of baseball, the American League, in order to increase scoring, adopted a rule in 1973 that a team can have another player bat in place of the pitcher, who is generally the weakest hitter on the team.

The National League did not adopt the rule.

I sided with the National League stance and argued that the pitcher was part of the team and should rightfully have a turn at bat; also, it was ridiculous for the two leagues to play with different rules.

Dad, a lifelong baseball fan, loved it.

CHRIS'S CHOICE

In '89, at Threshold, I had to choose a major. To help make that decision, the school gave me an occupational consult.

I rated high on patience and compassion. As a result, the fields of elder care and childcare were recommended.

Dad advised, totally straight-faced, that since I spent so much time with actors, who are basically spoiled, self-centered children, I should go into childcare.

After we laughed over that one, he reminded me that I had also spent a lot of time over the years tending to my ailing grandfather.

Christmas with Grandpa Raymond.

I thought: *Well, the elderly live at a slower pace, with physical and mental struggles, much like me.*

I chose elder care, the field in which I eventually got my AA degree.

CHRIS LEARNS TO SKI, PART 4

In 1988, my parents transferred me to Colorado Mountain College in Glenwood Springs, Colorado. The college promised that they had a learning lab for adults with an LD.

The bad news is: Colorado mountains. Snow up the wazoo.

Skiing.

Skiing!

Do you see the pattern? Vermont.

Colorado.

My parents tried to kill me.

WHEN E.F. HUTTON TALKS...

One good thing at Colorado Mountain College was that I got to co-direct a play with Tom Cochran, a wonderful theater teacher.

He told me, "Chris, actors are going to trust you because you understand theater, understand the vernacular, understand the process."

At the first table read of a play we were going to perform, Studs Terkel's *Working*, Tom advised the cast that if they didn't listen to me, they were idiots. "You know who his father is?" he asked, and let the question hover there before he answered, "Harvey Korman."

It was like an E.F. Hutton commercial. Everybody turned their attention from their script to me.

I detected some skepticism.

I wanted to yell, "*Hey*, just 'cause my father cross-dresses on television, it's to earn a living! He's a Shakespearian-trained actor!"

DAD TAKES A BOW

By 1985, after 13 years of co-hosting the Frostig golf tournament with me, Dad's interest started to wane.

There were a number of reasons.

Frostig had begun sticking him with bills for the event, rather than deducting those expenses from the fund-raiser total, which included entry fees, donations, auctions, and silent auctions. At first, Dad was a good sport about it, but after a while he felt enough was enough.

Another thing he was tired of was having to do the networking; i.e. rounding up the celebrities and making sure they showed up, and, if a last-minute professional job interfered with their appearance at the tourney, quickly enlisting a replacement.

Then there were the celebrities themselves who could be a major pain in the ass. As celebrities are known to do.

For example, a certain celebrity, let's call him Donald Duck, asked to go on first.

Dad explained that he'd already promised that position to another celeb, let's call her Minnie Mouse, but Mr. Duck could go second.

Of course, Mr. Duck wasn't comfortable with that, because, as he argued, "The reality is, I'm much more famous than she is. I should be the opener."

Dad was good at smoothing ruffled egos. "Yes, I agree that you're a bigger star, but I already promised her the opening slot."

"Hmmmm. Well, maybe I should close the show. You know, save the best for last. Yeah, I could do that."

"The thing is, I already gave the closing slot to Buddy Hackett."

"*Buddy Hackett?* Is he still *alive?*"

"Buddy is a dear friend of mine."

"Sorry, but I don't think that Borscht-belt Jewie-humor is gonna go over well with your WASPy golf crowd."

"Jewie-humor? I'm Jewish."

"So am I."

"Since when?"

"Oh shit, you know what? I just checked my appointment book. I completely forgot, I'm signed on to tape a *Bowling for Dollars* episode that night. Sorry, Harvey, maybe next year."

CHRIS TO THE RESCUE

You get the idea. Instead of the event being a fund-raiser for Frostig, it it had become an ego-trip for various celebs.

Before agreeing to appear, these people first had to know, "Who's gonna be in the audience that night?" or "How is this going to advance my career?"

And Dad was sick of it.

"Chris," he said, "you've been co-hosting this thing for 13 years, it's time to step up to the plate."

My impression was that Dad, more than souring on the thing, wanted me to take command. Despite my LD and speech problems, he felt I was capable of handling the event, plus it would be a huge psychological step for me to take responsibility for the tournament, to own it.

I did.

For the next nine years, I either hosted by myself or snared a celebrity like Frankie Avalon to co-host.

I would have gone on doing the tourney till I was 100 years old or dead, but at some point the Frostig golf tournament committee decided they were not making as much as they should be. Instead, they wanted to do in-house events.

Over and out.

CAROL, CARL, WHOOPI, AND ROBIN

That would be *Burnett, Reiner, Goldberg, and Williams*, a 1987 ABC-TV show about the history of laughter. It was directed by my Dad. Of course, he'd worked with Carl and Carol on the Burnett show but never with Whoopi or Robin.

I brought Scott to the taping. Unlike a lot of other people who were around my father and kissed-up to him, Scott was always very respectful, always addressed him as "Mr. Korman," and never gushed, "Ooh, can I see your Emmy Awards?"

Dad really liked him.

Scott and I sat in the front row with the invited audience.

During a break between skits, I turned to Scott. "Dad really didn't want to do this *at all*."

"How come?"

"Robin Williams. He's so brilliant that Dad was intimidated to work with him."

A guy sitting behind us must have overheard our conversation because he tapped me on the shoulder and, when I turned around, he said, "You're crazy."

"Thank you, yes I am, but who are you?"

"I'm Robin's agent. And the real story is, Robin was scared shitless to work with your father."

"Really? Why?"

"Harvey Korman is an icon in this business, a measuring stick for comedy."

That was a mind-blower, that Robin Williams revered my father, was actually afraid of him.

Wow.

After the taping, I took Scott backstage with me.

Robin was talking to Whoopie, but as soon as he saw me he said, "You have gotta be Harvey's son!"

I said, "Why?"

"'Cause nobody else has that shnozz."

Whoopi jumped on him, "I wouldn't talk about other people's noses, Robin. I mean, you are one hairy son-of-a-bitch."

MEL BROOKS

For *Blazing Saddles*, Mel Brooks offered the role of Hedley Lamarr to Gene Wilder who turned it down in favor of playing the Waco Kid.

Mel then offered the part to Carl Reiner—who now denies that allegation—but Carl recommended Dad.

The rest is history.

My father hit a new high in his career as the evil Hedley Lamarr.

Mel said that Dad was the finest comedic actor he ever worked with and promptly cast him in *High Anxiety*.

I was 10 years old and sufficiently well-behaved to be invited to the set for the shoot.

I still recall seeing Dad locked in chains, in a closet, with Cloris Leachman. Oh my God, an image I can never erase from my mind.

AKU, DAY 1

There was a notorious Hawaiian radio disk jockey named Hal Lewis, known as J. Akuhead Pupuli, or simply Aku, who died of cancer in 1983. Upon his death, the station manager read, on air, a note Aku had written before his death.

> Folks, the news is, I didn't make it. Last week I went to Queen's [Hospital] for a nuclear medicine radioactive scan which showed the damn cancer had spread to the left lung, and I'm in the group.
>
> Like I said, I didn't make it. Now hold on. It's a sad piece of news and I'm sorry to lay it on you this way, but for some reason, I feel up about it rather than down. After all, at age 66, I've had a damn good life.

Aku had a best friend/golf-buddy named Danny Arnold, who created/wrote/produced Barney Miller, That Girl, and Bewitched. After Aku died, Danny decided to honor him by setting up an annual golf tournament to raise money for cancer research.

So it was that in 1985, to celebrate my 18th birthday, Dad took me, along with his second wife Debbie and her parents, to Maui for the Second Annual Hal (Aku) Lewis Celebrity Golf Tournament.

To top it off, Hawaii had just lowered the legal drinking age from 21 to 18. Yes! I was in my glory!

For the occasion, Danny had flown in some of Hollywood's top stars on a private chartered jet.

Our first morning there, breakfast, Dad and I sat at one of those semi-circular half-booths; I faced the buffet table, where I could see everybody who entered and lined up for food.

None other than Burt Lancaster came off the line with a plate of food in his hand. He looked around, spotted us, and came straight for our table.

I immediately thought, Chew-chew-chew, Chris, chew-and-swallow, the last thing you want to do is spit your Spanish omelet all over Burt Lancaster.

Then I whispered to Dad, "Burt Lancaster is coming over."

"Why?"

"I don't know. You want me to ask him?"

"Yeah."

"No. You ask him."

Burt stopped at our table.

"Harvey?" he said.

"Burt?" Dad answered.

"What are you doing here?"

"I was invited to the golf tournament."

"Oh. Me, too."

Silence. Then, "This is my son, Chris."

"Hi, Chris."

"Hi, Burt."

Dad was clearly freaked out; for the next five seconds no one said a word.

Then I slid over and asked Burt to join us.

He sat and placed his plate on the table. Scrambled eggs, bacon, toast, home-fries, one pancake.

Dad was now on one side of me, Burt on the other side. I froze; mostly, I didn't want to say anything stupid.

I knew that neither did Dad. Burt just wolfed his food down.

After a minute or so, he said to Dad, "Sorry to eat so fast, but I have to be on hole twelve at nine-thirty, and I just wanted to meet you."

"Pardon?"

"I watched your show every Saturday night. You're wonderful." Dad was astounded, could barely speak.

He said, "Burt, you're a great actor, a serious actor, a movie star. I'm some schmuck who flounced around in women's clothing."

"Harvey, I don't think you appreciate how good you are. Everybody in the business watches everything you're in. You do things that we can't do."

"Cross-dress?" Burt turned to me.

"Chris, your father is a brilliant actor. He creates these incredibly believable human characters. On live television, no less."

Dad set his fork down and just stared at Burt.

"Guys," Burt said, and stood. "I have to run. Harvey, it was an honor to meet you."

He and Dad shook hands. Burt and I shook hands. "See ya on the links," he said and headed out.

Dad and I stared at each other, flabbergasted.

AKU, DAY 2

The tournament's sponsor Danny Arnold, who, besides his TV credits, also co-wrote a Dean Martin and Jerry Lewis movie, appropriately titled, *The Caddy*.

I knew that Jerry had recently undergone his second triple bypass.

I did not know that he was here at the tourney nor that he and Dad knew each other.

During breakfast, Jerry walked into the dining room wearing one of his typical V-neck sweaters over a candy-striped dress shirt. Very elegant.

Elegant, except for a lollipop stuck in his nose and another one in his mouth.

He bypassed the buffet table and came right over to Dad and me. Dad stood to greet him and they hugged like long-lost pals.

My mind was spinning: Yesterday, Burt Lancaster. Today, Jerry Lewis.

Somebody pinch me.

Dad said, "Jerry, this is my son, Chris."

Before I could say, "Pleased to meet you," or anything at all, Dad said, "Chris does a terrific imitation of you."

Oh shit.

I looked around for a hole I could crawl into. No holes.

Dad and Jerry waited. I pleaded stage-fright.

ALL THAT JAZZ

The final day of the tournament was to be a golf scramble: two-person teams, where each player hits a tee shot on every hole, with the follow-up shot taken from the best lie. It's more about fun than winning.

I was in a golf cart when I spotted Joe Williams just ahead of me.

For those who aren't into jazz, Joe Williams was one of the greatest jazz singers of all time. He sang with the Count Basie Orchestra, the Lionel Hampton Orchestra, and several combos. He also acted, playing Clare Huxtable's father on *The Cosby Show*.

Dad and I both love jazz, so, of course, I was not going to pass up an opportunity to say hello to him.

I went over and introduced myself.

"Hi, Mr. Williams, I'm Chris Korman. Sorry to bother you, but I'm a big fan of yours. My dad has all your records and we listen to you all the time."

He shook my hand. "Pleased to meet you Chris. Is your dad playing in the tournament?"

"Yes." I pointed to a nearby golf cart. "That's him over there."

"Whoa," he said, and got a huge smile across his face, "Your father is Harvey Korman?"

"Yes."

Next thing I know, Joe and I are walking over to Dad.

Of course, he recognized Joe immediately, and immediately shot me a look I was familiar with, the look that said, "Oh God, Chris, what have you done now?"

They introduced each other and slid into that Mutual Admiration Society thing that always blew my father away, because he was so insecure about his work that when someone he truly admired also admired him, he totally lost it.

Dad apologized to Joe on behalf of his rude son for intruding on Joe's time.

Joe defended me. "Harvey, your son was extremely polite. You must be a very proud papa."

Wow, I couldn't believe that endorsement.

We all shook hands, Joe headed back to his teammate, and I was about to return to my own cart when Dad slapped me on the back of my head.

"Why'd you bother Joe Williams for? He's probably preoccupied with the tournament."

"I'm sorry, Dad, but I'm not gonna pass up an opportunity to meet the greatest jazz singer ever."

"Hmm. Okay. But don't make a habit of it."

"Besides, he wanted to meet you."

Dad thought that over for a few seconds, then said, "Chris, you did good."

"Thanks. I know."

ADVENTURES WITH DAD

My father was often spacey when it came to remembering names and faces. Whenever we were out in public, my job was to keep track of people he had worked with, or people he hadn't worked with but should recognize. Despite my LD, I was his walking talking Wikipedia/IMDb.

In fact, I sometimes wondered if that's why he took me places: somebody would mention an event or an appearance and he'd whisper to me, *What year was that? How old was I? Did I have hair? Was I married to your mother?*

And so, one afternoon in 2005, when we entered a Santa Monica coffee shop—the Coffee Bean and Tea Leaf—I leaned closer to him and whispered, "There's Jennifer Grey sitting by the window."

"Who?"

"Joel Grey's daughter." "Uh…"

"You did a skit with him on the Burnett show."

"Right."

"But don't say anything about her nose."

(After starring in *Ferris Bueller's Day Off* and *Dirty Dancing*, Jennifer got a nosejob, which may or may not have sunk her career.)

Dad went right over to her.

I held my breath, hoping he wouldn't tell any nose jokes.

Thank God, he just introduced himself and said, "I loved working with your father, I hope he's well, and please send him my best regards."

By then, I'd spotted an empty table and made a bee-line for it.

On the way, Dad noticed that Michelle Pfeiffer was at another table. I crossed my fingers and hoped that Dad wouldn't go up to her.

But…

ADVENTURES WITH DAD 2

After Dad completed his chit-chat with Jennifer Grey, he looked around the room, saw me, and sat down at the table I'd grabbed.

"Chris, I need you to do me a favor."

"Okay."

He typically didn't want to be recognized in public, so I figured he was going to ask me to walk to the cashier, place our order, and bring it back to the table.

Instead, he said, "Go over to the cashier and say, loud, 'Harvey Korman, four-time Emmy Award winner *and* a Golden Globe winner from the Carol Burnett show wants a maple scone and a double latte.'"

I stared at him like he'd gone crazy. "Why would I do that?"

"Because Michelle Pfeiffer is sitting right over there."

Uh-oh, too late.

I played dumb: "So?"

"Chris, she's married to David Kelley."

Of course, I knew that David E. Kelley was the TV writer/producer who had created *L.A. Law, Ally McBeal*, and, currently, *Boston Legal*.

I shrugged, "So?"

"I want to be on *Boston Legal*."

"Don't you have, like, an agent or a manager, for that stuff?"

"It's not how the business works, Chris. Agents and managers are good for negotiating contracts, but first you gotta get the job. And that part is all about friendships. As they say, it's who you know."

At this point in his career, 1985, Dad was "between jobs": No matter how many years an actor has been in the business, no matter how successful, any time they're *between jobs* they become convinced that they're never ever going to work again.

So it was with Dad.

"Go on, Chris."

"I'm not doing that."

He was plenty pissed.

For a while he fumed, then he sulked, then he came to his senses, or so I thought.

"I'm sorry, Chris, you're right. What was I thinking?"

"You were thinking you'd make me look like an idiot so you could maybe get a job."

He nodded, "That's how you know you've hit rock bottom, when you try to pimp your son out."

Rock bottom? I hadn't sensed he was that seriously down in the dumps. Now I felt bad.

But before I could say, "Okay, I'll give it a shot," he was on his feet and headed for the counter.

Oh shit, I realized, *he's gonna do it himself.*

I did not want this performance embedded in my brain. As he joined the lengthy line of customers waiting to place their order, I quickly stood, placed my jacket on a seat to hold our table, and headed for the men's room.

There was another guy in there, at the sink, combing his hair in the mirror. I didn't have to pee, but I didn't want to look like I was loitering in the loo, so I went to the urinal, unzipped, and waited for the guy to leave.

He didn't. He just stood at the mirror, endlessly combing and re-combing his hair. Probably an actor.

Eventually, I zipped up, washed my hands, dried them on a paper towel, and left.

I'd hoped to see Dad seated at our table by then, with our coffee and scones, but no: I'd arrived just in time for his dramatic declaration.

"Two vanilla scones and two double lattes," he said, then added in a stage whisper, "The name is *Harvey Korman*."

In case you don't know, a stage whisper is an actor's whispered line from the stage, a whisper that carries clearly all the way up to the third balcony.

There was no use trying to hide. I went over and waited with him to help carry our order.

And then Michelle Pfeiffer approached.

"Harvey!" she said. "Sorry I didn't see you come in. How are you?"

Dad acted shocked. "Michelle! What a surprise!"

At that point, I turned and beat a hasty retreat. The last thing I heard was Dad say, "My son, Chris, he's incredibly shy about meeting new people."

Did Michelle go home and tell her husband, "Oh my God, I ran into Harvey Korman today at the Coffee Bean. He's such a wonderful actor. You must cast him on *Chicago Hope!*"

Maybe, maybe not.

Did Dad ever get onto *Boston Legal* or any of David Kelley's other shows? If he did, I was not about to watch that episode.

P.S.: I just did a search on Google, Wikipedia, and IMDb; Dad was never on a David E. Kelley show.

CHRIS GOES TO CAMP

There was a summer camp, the Idyllwild School of Music and Arts (ISOMATA). They had two week sessions and Dad signed me up for a session. I don't remember what plays we performed, though we also wrote our own.

I loved the camp so much that Dad signed me up for the following year. The coolest thing was when he drove me there and dropped me off. Everyone remembered me from last year and greeted us: "Hi, Chris!" "Hi, Chris!" "Hi, Chris's Dad!" That made me feel great.

Dad pretended to be miffed that it wasn't "Oh my God, *Harvey Korman!*" He griped, "You're the big cheese around here, aren't you? I'm glad people like you for you and not for who I am. I'm gonna leave now, drive straight to McDonald's, grab a big Mac, and cruise on back to LA. Have fun, Chrissy."

"Chrissy" let me know how happy he felt that I was recognized for myself.

THRESHOLD ACADEMY

"Transforming lives by challenging perceived limits and conquering them."
https://www.thresholdacademy.com/

In the summer of '89, I worked with Dad on a TV series, a sitcom that Mel Brooks and Alan Spencer created for him, *The Nutt House*.

I appeared as an extra in some scenes and also carried out various production jobs. For three months, I was up almost every morning by four a.m., and often toiled till late at night.

As a result, I earned over $3,000.

At summer's end, I was to start a three-year program at Threshold Academy in Cambridge, Mass.; a program for high-functioning adults with learning disabilities.

Dad met with the teacher in charge of the independent living program, who told him that the school would set up a bank account for every student, but no more than $500 in the account.

When Dad heard that, he went nuts.

"*Five hundred dollars?* That's *it?*"

"Sorry, Mr. Korman, it's a school rule."

"My son worked his ass off, and now you're telling me he can't touch his money."

"He can access five hundred dollars of it. As I said—"

"—Yeah, it's a school rule. So my son will be penalized because he has a strong work ethic."

"I'm sure you can understand that if we make an exception for Chris, it's not fair to the other students."

"*Life* isn't fair. I think *that's* a good lesson for your students." "We're trying to instill a sense of fiscal responsibility."

"Oh, you mean like how to budget for going to see a movie and buying a box of Raisinets? What about rent, mortgages, car payments, health insurance? How are they going to learn to handle large amounts of money if they don't start early?"

"There are some lessons best learned in the home, explained by their parents."

"Oh, so we should teach our kids 'Don't worry, Mommy and Daddy will take care of those car payments'?"

Needless to say, Dad lost that argument.

FINANCIAL MODEL

The funny thing about my father's argument with the principal was that Dad's own checkbook looked like a football team's playbook as marked up by a dyslexic coach with a large box of crayons.

But I well understood his point: He grew up poor and never really learned about financial ins and outs; he had a business manager who handled his money.

Dad's concern that I learn these essentials was well-founded.

MILKING IT

At the Threshold orientation weekend, Dad and I made an unpleasant discovery: the Disney educational video I was featured in at age 15, whose title I couldn't even remember (*In the Mind's Eye? Through the Mind's Eye?*) was being used there, seven years later, as part of the curriculum in a class called "The Understanding of Learning Disabilities."

The thrust of the class was: If you have an LD, don't use it as crutch. Which raised all sorts of moral and practical questions. My best friend Scott Marshall invariably used his cerebral palsy as a crutch, so to speak.

Remember how, in his wheelchair, we cut to the front of long lines at Disneyland?

Remember when I scolded him, "Scott, you exploited your handicap!" And he told me, "Chris, you milk it where you can milk it."

I never did that.

I mean, I don't think I ever did that. Oh wait.

Shit.

I mean, I don't think I ever exploited my learning disability; I wouldn't even know how to do that.

But, as a prosecuting attorney might demand: "Chris, are you now or have you ever exploited your father's name and fame for your own ends?"

A fair question.

Would you be reading this if I was just some schlub with an LD instead of Harvey Korman's son?

Hmmm...

All right, Your Honor, guilty as charged. Yes, I milk it where I can milk it. Thanks, Scott.

THAT DAMNED DISNEY VIDEO AGAIN

When Dad and I found out that my future schoolmates would already know me as the son of a celebrity, from that Disney video, we were upset and pissed off.

I met with the school's director. She said, "Chris, I understand your feelings in this regard, but it's important that you establish yourself here on your own merits, your own identity."

"But you've already sandbagged me with that video. It's hypocritical of you to to expect me to establish my own identity after you outed me."

She considered that.

"By the way," I asked, "did you watch the video?"

"Yes. And I felt you were very brave to speak out as you did. Brave, and very convincing. That's why we chose to use the video as a pedagogical device. Not because of your famous father."

Maybe so, but still, my first month at Threshold, many of my classmates acted like I was born with a silver spoon up my ass.

They were unsparing:

"Ooh, a Disney star!"

"Hey Chris, do the Hollywood strut!"

"Tell us about all your celebrity friends!"

But little by little, they came around, and I became a normal Threshold student.

Normal for Threshold, at any rate.

But the experience taught me a lesson: If you're in the public eye, you need a thick skin.

CO-ED COLLEGE

Despite Dad's misgivings about the $500 maximum account each student could have, the school did teach us many of the practical everyday tasks that Dad was so concerned about: How to open a bank account, make deposits, pay bills with checks, and reconcile the balance.

Academically, we had to choose a specialty. I chose elder care. To satisfy that requirement, I worked as an apprentice at an adult daycare center in Boston.

Oh, and the school used the facilities of Lesley College, which at the time was an all-girls school, though we had nothing to do with each other. The Lesley girls were probably happy about that as they surely thought we were a bunch of Nutt cases.

For my part, I worried that if I couldn't get a date at an all-girl's college, I'd never get married.

DOYLESTOWN

In 1985, Mom and George moved to Pipersville, Pennsylvania, a mere 80 miles from Manhattan.

They both loved being near New York City, with all its Broadway and off-Broadway theaters. Plus, Doylestown is in Bucks County, home to the Bucks County Playhouse. So there were ample opportunities for work and teaching.

Another factor was George's mother, who lived in Connecticut. She was not in good health and George wanted to be geographically closer to her than out in LA.

In '92, I graduated from Threshold.

Dad and Maria with me.

After graduation, I decided to remain on the East Coast with Mom and George.

Although, size-wise, Pipersville was on a par with tiny little Putney, Vermont—a grocery store, a bank, a bar, a gas station—since I didn't drive, the town's size worked to my advantage: I could easily walk wherever I needed to.

Like, to my new job at Pine Run Nursing Home.

At Pine Run, I performed several different functions. I made beds, worked in the dining room, transferred patients into and out of their wheelchairs, helped nurses, ran some activities, played checkers with the patients, etc.

I loved it. It was a great job.

And I met a fellow worker there, let's call her Joan.

Joan and I started dating, which led to a serious relationship. I was 24 and hadn't ever been in a serious relationship.

A TALK WITH DAD

One night, I called Dad and during our conversation told him I was seeing someone.

"Terrific," he said, "tell me about her."

"Her name is Joan, she works with me at Pine Run. She's divorced, she's lots of fun, and I really like her."

"She's divorced?" "Yeah."

"How old is she?" "Thirty-four."

"Chris, she's ten years older than you." "Wow, you did the math, Dad, very good!" "So, you like older women?"

"I like *this* older woman."

"Does she know you're my son?" "Of course!"

He was quiet for a minute.

I chimed in, "I know what you're thinking, that she's using me to get to you. Do you know how insulting that is?"

"I just don't wanna see you get hurt. There are people out there, people you'll encounter, who will try to use you, manipulate you."

"Because I'm your son and you're rich and famous."

"I'm sorry to say it, Chris, but that's the way some people are."

SUGAR BABY?

After that talk with Dad, I stewed for a while, angry at him.

But was he right?

Was Joan interested in me only because my dad was rich and famous?

The question nagged at me and, in the end, made me question the relationship.

Sadly, we broke up.

Y&R

Whenever I was out in LA visiting Dad, every weekday afternoon, promptly at 12:25, I disappeared into my bedroom.

One day, Dad followed me in, saw me turn the TV on, and asked what I was going to watch.

"*The Young and the Restless.*"

"You're gonna watch a s*oap opera?*"

I understood his incredulity. There's a show business pecking order—or at least there used to be. At the top of the heap is Broadway; then, movies, then prime-time television, and last, way down there at the bottom, soap operas.

"Yes, Dad, I'm going to watch a soap opera."

"Why?"

"I like it. Plus, half the crew from the Burnett show now work on this one."

Dad became curious enough to stand there and watch the opening. Earlier in the year, *Y&R* started to display the cast names over the opening theme music. When the name "Brenda Dickson" came on, Dad went, "*Wait! Who?*"

"Brenda Dickson."

"I dated that crazy bitch," he said. "One time, she grabbed me by the family jewels."

"*What?*"

"Yeah. We were at a party, I was standing, talking to some people, and she snuck up behind me, reached around, and grabbed my balls."

"Did I really need to know that? You've kinda ruined my Young and the Restless experience. Thanks."

"What's her character?"

"She plays Jill Foster Abbott, a beautician—a raving lunatic who only wants a sugar daddy."

"*L'arte imita la vita.*"

"What?"

"Art imitates life."

"Shhh, it's starting."

And so he sat down and we watched the episode together.

CHRISTMAS CHEER

In 1996, I'd lived on the East Coast for ten years and hadn't spent a Christmas with Dad that whole time. Christmas and New Year's Eve I was with Mom and George. In January, after the holidays, I'd fly to LA for time with Dad.

But in '96, I was with my father for the entire Christmas-New Year's holiday week.

One day, we were driving around Santa Monica in the Lexus. (Yes, that hideous red Honda finally died.) He'd been quiet for a while. I looked at him and saw a certain expression he sometimes wore, a combination of anxiety and depression.

That look I came to associate as a time when he was "between jobs." i.e. unemployed. As with many insecure actors (most? all?), he was convinced that no one would ever hire him for a project, that he'd never work again.

He normally dealt with his anxiety/depression by staying in his office and listening to opera, doing crossword puzzles, and calling his agent every half hour.

Thankfully, for him the time between jobs was always short; therefore, so were his bouts of bummed-out.

I said, "You look unhappy, Dad. You okay?"

When a child asks that question to a parent, the hoped-for answer is "I'm fine, thanks for asking."

Instead, he said, "I don't know how much longer I want to live."

My brain reeled: *What? I come out here for the holiday and THAT'S what you hit me with?* "I don't know how much longer I want to live?"

I said, "Oh, and a merry fucking Christmas to you, Dad!"

With that, he cracked up laughing. Uncontrollable laughter. He had to pull over to the side of the road and stop the car.

When he finally calmed down, he patted my leg and said, "Thank you, Chrissy."

I said, *I love you*, Dad. He said, *I love you too, Chrissy, now let's go eat.*

Merry fucking Christmas!

MATH

Another time I visited him, in the mid-'90s, Dad gave me $150 for the week, as an allowance.

"Okay," he'd say, "you have a hundred-and-fifty dollars to last you for five days. Tell me, how much can you spend per day?"

"Dad, this isn't a first-grade arithmetic test."

"Come on, how much?"

"The correct answer is fifty dollars a day."

"Right."

"Except that if I take my friend Brian to a movie, that's ten dollars each, another eight dollars each for popcorn and soda, lunch afterwards at McDonald's—not Spago's—Big Macs with cheese, medium fries, small Diet Cokes, comes to a grand total of fifty-nine dollars and change. Let's just say sixty. Which means," I concluded, "that I now have ninety dollars for the next four days, or *twenty-two dollars and fifty-cents per day*."

Dad furrowed his brow as he followed along.

"Okay, Chris, I see your point. If you need more money, call Norman, I'll let him know."

Norman Greenbaum was his accountant and business manager. When you grow up poor, as Dad did, and suddenly come into money, as Dad did, it's a good idea to have a business manager.

SQUEEZING BLOOD FROM A STONE (NOT!)

So, whenever I was on vacation, if I needed money, I just asked. He never wanted to say no to his children, never wanted to be the heavy.

Weird as this may sound, I actually got in an argument with him, where I challenged him to say *NO, I'm not giving you another dime!*

"I can't do that, Chris. I..."

Then he started crying. "I feel like... I failed you. I should have been... tougher. I only wanted... to be a good dad."

I hugged him.

"It's okay. You're a great dad. I love you."

A DAY IN THE LIFE

Dad's morning ritual consisted of a bagel with cream cheese, a pot of coffee, and the *LA Times*.

When I arrived for breakfast, he'd have the sports page folded open on my place mat, with a marking-pen arrow pointed at Jim Murray's article.

That was his rule: you eat breakfast while you read Jim Murray and then you go about the rest of your day.

In the evening, if there was a Dodger game on that we were not going to the stadium for, we'd sit at the bar, drink beer, eat peanuts, and watch the game on TV.

Dad hated the television announcer, so he'd mute the TV and we'd listen to the broadcast on the radio, to Vin Scully, long-time voice of the Dodgers, and close friend of my father's.

FAN MAIL

Dad had a huge cardboard box where he "stored" his fan mail.

At some point, my sister Maria was placed in charge of answering those letters. They were all pretty much the same: "Dear Harvey, you're wonderful!" "Dear Harvey, you are so talented!" "Dear Harvey, you brought so much joy into our lives over the years."

And then the inevitable request for an autographed photo; long after the Burnett show went off the air, Dad still had stacks of publicity photos of himself.

Maria wrote the actual reply, if needed. I placed her reply in the fan's self-addressed, stamped envelope along with Dad's autographed photo.

One day, finally, she ran out of those publicity photos that CBS had paid for.

I broke the news to him: "Dad, you need to do another photo session."

"Really? You mean rent a studio, hire a photographer, a lighting person, a stylist, a hair-and-makeup specialist, and a wardrobe person. No, Chris, I'm not gonna spend another fucking dime on photos of myself. Fuck it."

Thereafter, every piece of fan mail was tossed unopened into that cardboard box. I have no idea where it is today or how many unopened envelopes it contains or if Dad's fans are still waiting, twenty years later, for that autographed photo of their idol.

INCOGNITO

As a young man, I developed acne on my chest and shoulders, necessitating frequent trips to the dermatologist; in this case, Doctor Arnold Klein, the Beverly Hills dermatologist-to-the-stars. (In fact, Dr. Klein's head nurse, Debbie Rowe, married one of his patients, Michael Jackson.)

As soon as we arrived for my appointment, I went to the restroom. Dad sat in the waiting room, picked up a magazine, and buried his face in it.

When I returned to the waiting room, I sat between him and a woman patient.

The woman leaned over to me and whispered, "Is that Harvey Korman?"

Standard Operating Procedure: "Chris, if we're out together and someone asks you, 'Is that Harvey Korman'? You say, 'No.'"

I turned to the woman and said, "Who?"

"Harvey Korman," she repeated.

"Oh. No."

A few minutes later, the nurse popped into the room: "Chris, come on in." As I stood up, she added, "Harvey, nice to see you."

The woman burst out, "I knew it! I knew it!" I hurried inside, totally embarrassed.

Our next appointment was even worse: he affected a German accent. The waiting room was half full. As soon as we sat down, he said, "Chris, vill you pleaze hend me zat magazine?"

And after I handed it to him, *"Danke schön."*

It was all I could do to not burst out laughing.

LEAVING TOWN

For eight years—'92-2000—I lived in Doylestown, PA, a very small step up, size-wise, from Pipersville.

Mom and George separated and divorced.

After a while, Mom moved to Baltimore, where she met and married Richard.

Eventually, I became burned out with menial jobs: the Bon-Ton Department Store; the Pine Run retirement home; Russell's 96 West restaurant.

Then I just said *fuckit* and moved to Baltimore.

TRISH

Soon after arriving in Baltimore, I met Trish on a dating website.

Many of the pictures I had posted were from Frostig golf tournaments, where I was in a tuxedo standing at a podium.

She posted: "Why are you always in a tuxedo? Are you the host at a fancy restaurant?"

Eventually, we met for coffee, and I explained that I wasn't the maître d' at a steak-house, that the tuxedo was for public speaking engagements having to do mostly with fundraising affairs for Frostig.

I added, "My current job is with the Baltimore Office of Community Conservation."

"What's that?"

"Uh, let's say you want to put a soup kitchen in your church, or maybe a hurricane struck down your house, our office helps provide funding. So I deal with lawyers, government officials, not-for-profits, various organizations."

Trish thought that was cool. She herself was an accountant, but a frustrated one; deep down, she wanted to be an artist.

We fell in love and soon were spending every weekend together.

We decided to marry at this small chapel in Towson, MD. I told my boss at work that I would need a day off for the occasion.

Trish's Dad, Thomas, was there for the Big Day.

Moments after Trish and I were officially wed, we came down to the lobby on the elevator. As the elevator doors opened, there were 35 people standing there, yelling, "Congratulations, Chris and Trish!"

And then each and every one of them started blowing bubbles. Bubbles filled the entire lobby like on a really bad Lawrence Welk show.

Bubbles.

GOOD NEWS, DAD!

My father was over the moon when I told him Trish and I got married.

Yes, of course, he was happy for us, but his delight had a practical basis as well.

"Chris, you have no idea how much I appreciate you getting married in civil court. You just saved me a hundred thousand dollars!"

He meant the cost of having to throw a big Hollywood-style wedding. "Plus," he went on, "you saved me from having to murder your mother and sisters."

Because the women would have strong opinions on the wedding arrangements, opinions that would certainly differ from Dad's.

Two birds with one stone.

ANALYZE THIS

A Hollywood truism: the minute you fully commit to a family vacation—or a project you're only so-so on—the opportunity of a lifetime presents itself.

Dad and Tim had put together this two-man show, mixing in some recycled skits from *The Carol Burnett Show* with some original material. They traveled across the country performing in theaters, country clubs, casinos, anyplace that would guarantee a payday.

While they were developing the act, and already had venues lined up, Dad bumped into Billy Crystal at a Hollywood Stars event at Dodger Stadium. Billy asked Dad to play Billy's father in a film with Robert De Niro called *Analyze This*.

The thing is, Dad was always uncomfortable working with people he hadn't worked with before; he'd never worked with Billy Crystal, and certainly not with Robert De Niro.

He turned it down.

BASKETBALL JONES

May 26 2002.

The Los Angeles Lakers and Sacramento Kings were in the middle of NBA playoffs and I was in Las Vegas to celebrate my birthday—two days earlier—with Dad, who was in Vegas performing with Tim.

When it came to basketball, as with so many other areas outside of acting/baseball/food, my dad was a nincompoop. As often as I tried to explain the zone defense, he never could grasp it.

On this particular evening, while I watched the game on TV, Dad was notified for his half-hour call, which meant he had thirty minutes to finish dressing; at that point, one of the hotel's security people would pick him up and escort him down to the theater through the service area and kitchen.

Okay, so the Lakers are down by 25 points. *The 2002 LA Lakers*. We're talking Kobe Bryant, Shaquille O'Neal, Jannero Pargo, Rick Fox, and Robert Horry, coached by the great Phil Jackson.

Suddenly, the Lakers started to score. And each time they scored, I let out a cheer.

And each time I cheered Dad came racing into the room. It was the first time I ever saw him get excited about a Lakers game.

Now he was mostly dressed for his performance, in a tuxedo, but he still hadn't attached the studs for his dress shirt.

"Dad, didn't you get your half-hour call, like, five minutes ago?"

"Yeah-yeah, plenty of time."

"Well you better finish dressing."

"Who's the big guy?"

"Shaquille O'Neal."

"How tall is he?"

"Shaq is seven-foot-one, and wears a size 22 shoe."

"Damn! Why does he keep missing the basket?"

"He's not good at free throws. Other teams know that, so they foul him a lot. It's a strategy called Hack the Shaq."

"Huh."

"Dad! Get dressed!"

He went back into his bedroom, but two minutes later, Kobe sank a three-pointer. I yelled *"YES!"* and Dad came running back in.

"What happened?"

"Kobe sank one from the perimeter."

"Where's the perimeter?"

I pointed. "That circle there."

Then I noticed that he still didn't have his cufflinks on and was missing a stud.

"Dad, you now have twenty minutes."

"I can't find my other stud."

I glanced around and saw something small and shiny on the floor by the bedroom door. I went over, picked up the stud, and handed it to him.

He ran back into his bedroom.

I tried not to yell out anymore, but it was hard to sit there silently as the Lakers roared back from 25 points down.

And then Shaq blocked a Kings shot and tossed it way down-court to Kobe for an easy layup.

"*Oh my god!*" I yelled.

Dad ran back in.

"What? *What?*"

"We're only down by nine points now. And your security guy will be here in fifteen minutes."

He ran back into his bedroom.

I tried to control myself but pretty soon we were only five points down and I lost it, screaming at the top of my lungs. Of course, Dad tore back in and became just as excited as I was. Any time the Lakers scored or the Kings missed a shot and we got the rebound, we both screamed.

SAN DIEGO

In 2005, four years after our son Scott was born, we moved to San Diego so he could get to know his grandfather.

I got a job at Sea World.

When Tim and Dad brought their show to the Pala Casino, on the Pala Indian Reservation near San Diego, Dad invited the three of us to a performance there.

We dressed Scott in a cute little tuxedo.

As we entered the theater, a security guard stopped us and informed us that children were not allowed inside.

I said, "Would you like to tell that to my father?"

She looked around and said, "Who's your father?"

"Harvey Korman."

"Oh."

"Yeah, he asked us to bring our son because he thought it would be wonderful for his first grandson to see him perform."

"Of course. Right this way, please."

She led us to a corner table with a great view of the stage.

Scott doesn't have a memory of the event, but I do. At one point, when Dad left the stage to Tim alone, Scott turned to another audience member and said, "Don't worry, Harvey Korman is coming back. It's fine, don't worry."

Harvey and Tim in the Olden Days.

SEA WORLD

I worked security at Sea World: I was one of those dweebs in a safari suit who examined patrons' bags when they entered.

Really.

Besides the normal stuff, like food—they'd have to check those items in a locker—we had a guy try to bring in a gun.

"Whoa," I said, "you can't bring that in here."

"I'm a security guard."

"Not here. *I'm* the security guard here."

"It's okay, I'm licensed."

"Really? So are you planning to shoot a dolphin or a shark in case they jump out of the water?"

He checked his gun.

I worked there for seven months, during the high tourist season. The schedule was insane: some days I'd work a normal shift from, say, eight a.m. to three, then they'd switch me, with almost no warning, to a noon-to-eight shift.

I hated it.

A DEATH IN THE FAMILY

On May 29, 2008, Dad died.

I was still working at Sea World and asked my boss for a few days off to attend my father's funeral.

No one at Sea World knew I was Harvey Korman's son, but when I talked to the HR person about time off, she apparently had read the news about Dad's death and put two-and-two together regarding my last name.

"I'm sorry for your loss," she said, in all sincerity. But I detected a look in her eyes, a look I'd seen many many many times before: "Oh my God! It's Harvey Korman's son!"

IN MEMORIAM

My father's memorial was like a *Blazing Saddles/Carol Burnett Show* reunion. It was held in a small church in Santa Monica. Or maybe it wasn't a church, maybe it was more of an off-Broadway theater-in-the-round with spiritual overtones. I was too devastated to soak it all in.

I do know there were at least 300 people in attendance.

Even though I'd prepared Trish and Scott in advance for what to expect, it was still intimidating to them when stars like Steve Lawrence and Eydie Gorme introduced themselves and expressed their condolences.

I was able to stay calm through Mel Brooks' beautiful eulogy.

But then, via recording, Vin Scully spoke—spoke lovingly, emotionally—about my dad and baseball, about life and the rules.

At some point, I lost it. Broke down in sobs.

Yeah.

The Dodgers.

Baseball.

TV CONFIDENTIAL

Since 2016, I have been a producer on a radio talk show, *TV Confidential*, a show that "...directs itself primarily to the Baby Boomer, Generation X and senior markets." i.e. older folks for whom the name Harvey Korman is as familiar to them as Jennifer Lawrence or Matt Damon are to a younger audience.

The show is hosted by Ed Robertson, a terrific writer, journalist, and interviewer.

My job as producer is to round up guests.

For most of my employment there, I have been unpaid. What benefit, then, do I derive?

Basically, I get to reconnect with show business people who either knew my father personally, or worked with him, or were so enamored of his career that they will happily do Dad's son a favor by appearing as a guest on the show.

Am I being used for the clout the Korman name holds? Maybe.

But if so, the exploitation is upfront. I don't worry and wonder any more if this person or that person is being nice to me in order to get to my father.

He's gone.

TAKING IT ON THE ROAD

In 2017, I stumbled on the Learning Disabilities Association of America website (https://ldaamerica.org/) and emailed them to see if I could get involved in their program.

I noticed that they had an annual conference, so I asked about attending and perhaps saying a few words regarding my own LD experiences.

They replied that to address the next conference, I would have to submit a proposed topic along with a $25 fee.

I went ahead and submitted a proposal: "How Public Speaking and Speech Pathology Became a Valuable Tool in My Personal Development."

A wordy title, but I figured I could pare it down and make it catchier if I was accepted.

I was.

For weeks I worked on my speech, very much like in the old days: recording it, listening to the playback, refining, working on my diction, and revising.

The more I worked on it, the more excited I became. It felt like this was what I should be doing with my life, talking to families with an LD child, offering encouragement by example; not giving endless interviews to recite the same old anecdotes about Dad, Tim, Carol, and the sundry movie stars and professional athletes who entered my life because I was Harvey Korman's son.

So, I spoke about how important it is to create one's own niche, one's place in life, to have realistic expectations, and not try to live up to parental or societal expectations.

I spoke for an entire hour, but could have answered questions for another two hours.

SURPRISE!

After my presentation, I was mobbed by people who introduced themselves, congratulated me on my speech, gave me their business cards, made it a point to connect with me on social media, and hoped that I would have time to work on behalf of their own various organizations.

And the woman who is the head of the LDA gave me a big hug and said how terrific it was to have me there, especially because my father had been involved with the organization for several years.

Surprise-surprise!

"What? Really?"

"You didn't know that?"

"No. I had no idea."

"In fact, he was our national spokesman."

"What?"

"Yes. And we will always be grateful that he used his celebrity to advance our cause."

And then I had a flashback to a night in '82 or so, when my father appeared on the Johnny Carson show, and I was there in the Green Room, watching the interview on a monitor, and Dad mentioned that he was about to leave for Chicago on behalf of an organization that helped children with learning disabilities.

So that's where he kept disappearing to, traveling around the country on behalf of the LDAA.

And I thought he was just running out for Chinese food.

BALTIMORE

While in Baltimore for the conference, I was fortunate to spend some time with Mom and my sister Maria, neither of whom I'd seen for a while.

Maria, Mom and me in Baltimore.

All in all, the three-day LDAA affair was an uplifting experience.

I attended at least a dozen speeches and met many of the activists in the LD world, who readily invited me into that community.

For example, a woman named Carrie Fannin heard me speak. Later, we ran into each other in the lobby of the hotel. She congratulated me on my talk and introduced herself as the Executive Director of CHILD (Children's Institute for Learning Differences), in Seattle, Washington.

As we talked, I learned that there were actually people who did what I just did, but did it professionally: who traveled around the country—around the world—to speak about learning disabilities. There were folks who actually supported themselves while performing important work for the LD community.

Carrie insisted that I was a very empathetic speaker who could become a spokesperson for that community, particularly since I had grown up with an LD.

In some ways, the entire three days reminded me of my childhood at Frostig, of discovering I wasn't some freakish anomaly; that there was a whole community of folks just like me.

It was also wonderful to be treated as myself, Chris Korman, not as Harvey Korman's son.

At the end of the event, the LDAA Director urged me to write a book; a memoir, about how my learning disability had impacted my life.

She also welcomed me to return every year, either as an attendee or, preferably, as a speaker.

I promised her a book, and a return engagement.

TALKING IN CODE

During that Las Vegas trip, Trish, back home in Baltimore, was newly pregnant, so it would remain a secret, even from my father, until she reached the three-month mark.

Except that whenever I was on the phone with her, Dad was also in the room and eager to talk to her.

Of course, I couldn't ask any specific questions about her health. My end of the conversation was mostly, "How are you doing?" and "How's your mom?" and lots of "Uh-huh" and "Yeah." All through it, I shot cheerful smiles at Dad while being careful not to drop any clues about Trish's condition.

And baby makes three.

SIGNALS & SIGNS

On that same trip, Dad and Tim were going to do an interview with one of the tabloids, about Carrie Hamilton, Carol Burnett's daughter, who had recently died of cancer.

The interview was to take place in the Hilton's lounge; Dad asked me to hang out for the interview.

Of course, he had a secret agenda.

While the crew set up the lights and arranged the set, Dad let me in on the plan.

"Chris, I need you to kinda hang out in the corner over there and when I look like I'm gonna say something stupid, give me a signal."

I immediately understood. With Dad and Tim together in front of a camera, any kind of zany behavior might occur, which would be wildly inappropriate in discussing the premature death of Carol's daughter.

And since I knew my father pretty well, like, when he was about to say something stupid, a signal was a good idea.

Except for one thing.

"What kind of signal?" I asked.

"Oh, uh, maybe cough or clear your throat."

"What if I really have to cough?"

Dad thought about that for a minute, then came up with a baseball analogy.

"Okay, so you know how when the catcher signals the pitcher what kind of pitch to make and gives him a target?"

"Uh-huh."

"And then the pitcher returns the catcher a sign, like, he tugs his earlobe to mean 'Ooh, yeah, great idea.' Or he scratches his nose to say, 'Ugh, that sucks.'"

"So, you want me to... what?"

"Tug your earlobe if I'm doing fine and scratch your nose if I'm about to say something stupid."

I scratched my nose. He wasn't amused.

Tim and Dad sat next to each other on a sofa, across from the interviewer. Whenever my father was asked a question, he looked over at me for a prompt. Pretty soon, Tim caught on to the interaction but had no idea what it was about.

"What's going on?" he asked Dad.

"We're being interviewed, Tim."

"I mean, you know," and he nodded towards me. The interviewer turned to look; I smiled and waved.

"My son has tinnitus," Dad explained.

I scratched my nose in warning, but he ignored.

"So sometimes he has to tug on his ear to relieve the pressure. It's genetic." To prove his point, he tugged on his ear. "See?"

I scratched my nose like a madman.

LOVE

In 2003, Dad and Tim's show arrived in Baltimore. When it did, my sister Maria arranged for a dinner at a fancy restaurant where she knew the chef/owner.

It was here where Trish and Dad finally met.

Needless to say, after my father's issue with my ex-girlfriend Judy, I was scared shitless about what he would think of Trish.

My son Scott, a year-and-a-half old, in a highchair, was delighted with Dad's constant display of funny faces, peek-a-boo games, and general ridiculousness.

At some point, I excused myself and went to the restroom. Dad followed me.

"Chris, what are you so nervous about?"

"Remember when I was in Las Vegas for my birthday, and we watched a Lakers playoff game and you and Tim did that interview?"

"Sure."

"I couldn't tell you at the time, but Trish was pregnant."

"I know. You called me when Scott was born. I subtracted nine months and figured it out. Is that what you're nervous about?"

"No. I'm afraid you don't like her. That you think she's another gold-digger."

"Chris, you're a *putz*. I love her, she gave me my first grandchild."

Scott with his grandpa.

LUNCH

Dad and Anthony Hopkins became friendly. They each admired the other's work and ate lunch together several times.

If you've seen *The Silence of the Lambs* and *Blazing Saddles*, you'll understand what Dad meant when he informed me, after one such meeting, "Hannibal had Hedley for lunch."

Dad and Scott do brunch.

LOST

In 2005, Trish and I decided to move to Southern California so we could be close to Dad, especially so Scott could spend time with his grandfather. Los Angeles was too costly and inconvenient for us to live there. Instead, we decided to investigate San Diego as a possible destination.

A few months previous, I bought Trish an elegant and classyer' watch on a diamond-encrusted bracelet. Now, as we were about to leave our hotel room for the drive up to Los Angeles, she couldn't find the watch.

We opened every drawer in the room, looked under the bed and under every piece of furniture, took the bed apart and remade it, and searched through the pockets of every article of Trish's clothing.

Then we repeated the entire process. No watch.

Trish started to sob: "I can't believe it... the first piece of jewelry you bought me and... and... I lose it."

I held her. "Don't worry. We'll find it."

We drove the rental car up to Dad's house in Bel Air. For most of the two-hour trip, Trish sat there grim-faced and silent.

When we arrived at Dad's, she managed to greet him with a cheery smile, but I knew my father; he'd picked up on something amiss.

He took us out to lunch. I don't remember where.

During lunch, Trish continued to maintain a cheerful demeanor, but finally Dad said, "Guys, what's going on?"

Trish and I exchanged a look. I shrugged.

She said, "I'm sorry, Harvey. It's just... Chris bought me this beautiful piece of jewelry... a Bulova watch... and I... *I lost it.*"

"Hmm. Okay, here's what we're gonna do. Right after lunch, I'll drop you and Scott off at the house so he can take his nap, and Chris and I will go to this jewelry shop I know in Santa Monica, and buy you another watch."

"Thanks. Thanks so much, but the one Chris bought me had sentimental value. You can't replace it."

"I understand. But I hate to see my daughter-in-law unhappy. Please humor me on this."

She finally nodded, "Okay."

After we dropped Trish and Scott off at Dad's house, we drove out to Santa Monica. A jewelry store called Sarah Leonard Fine Jewelers.

As soon as we walked in, Leonard the owner, an elderly gent in shirt and tie, greeted Dad with a big hug, then turned to me.

"You must be Chris."

"How do you know?"

"Your father brags about you all the time. He's shown me pictures of you since you were a baby."

I was speechless.

Dad explained the situation to him, and I described every aspect of the lost watch, every stone, every color.

Leonard led us to a display case and selected a watch that closely matched the Bulova I'd bought Trish, except that this watch was even more beautiful.

And more expensive.

Leonard placed the watch on a velvet pillow and informed us that it was an Alexora, from the 1920's; platinum, with 2.19 carats worth of diamonds, and a 15-jewel manual-wind movement.

Price: $6,000. I gulped.

Dad saw the expression on my face. He asked Leonard to give us a moment, family conference.

As soon as we were alone, I said, "Dad, I can't afford six thousand dollars."

"I'm paying."

"Yeah, well it'll take me fifteen years to pay you back."

"Listen, it's a gift, from me to my daughter-in-law."

"But she's my *wife!*"

"And my *daughter-in-law!*"

Later, on the drive back to Bel Air, the argument continued, this time over who was going to present the watch to her.

Dad: "Listen, *putz*, she's my daughter-in-law! I'll give it to her."

With that, I grabbed for the bag with the watch.

He slapped my hand.

Long story short: he gave Trish the watch. She loved it.

I'd never seen my father so happy.

I wound up feeling pretty terrific that they both were so delighted.

GUESS WHAT

Before we drove up to Dad's, we'd shopped for a few items including a six-pack of small water bottles. Trish had torn open the plastic wrap and grabbed three bottles of water for the drive to LA.

Upon our return to San Diego, we opened the trunk to bring the rest of the water bottles up to our hotel room.

Lo and Behold!, there on the cardboard bottom of the water bottle case, was the Bulova watch I'd bought her!

Apparently, when she opened the case, the watch had snagged on the plastic and slid off her wrist.

I called Dad and explained what had happened.

"So we can return the watch you bought her."

"Are you fucking out of your mind? It's irrelevant that you found the watch."

"You want her to have both watches?"

"Putz, you miss the point. My daughter-in-law was hurt and miserable, and I didn't want to see her in pain."

That tells you everything about who my father was.

Dad, Scott, and me.

When Trish and I first starting dating I was trying to see if she could guess who my father was. I told her, "He was on the Carol Burnett Show, and he was the tall good looking one."

Trish said, "Lyle Waggoner?"

"No!"

"He was the funny one."

She said, "Tim Conway?"

"No!"

"He was a movie star."

Trish, "Dick Van Dyke?"

I laughed and said Harry Korman.

Trish said, "Oh, my mom said he was dead."

I laughed hard, I responded, "Just his career." Later on my Dad added, Just from the waist down.

LOVE

They say you can tell how much a person loves you by whether or not they pick you up at the airport.

Particularly, LAX.

Dad always picked me up.

But of course, he'd do it in typical Harvey Korman mode.

He'd hide behind a corner or pillar outside Arrivals until I emerged, then he'd surreptitiously follow me, like some third-rate Sam Spade, to the baggage claim area.

Eventually, I'd hear, *"Hey smuck, turn around!"*

And he'd pop out with a long-lost hug and kisses on both cheeks and forehead.

By the third time he pulled that act, when I got to baggage claim, I whirled around and yelled, "Hey you! *Stop following me!*"

PROTECTION

Dad took the concept of protecting his family to a near-paranoid extreme.

Every night before he went to bed he made a routine inspection of the entire house to be certain all the doors were locked, the windows shut, and the burglar alarm activated.

But it didn't stop there.

We had a fireplace. He'd get down on his hands and knees and peer up the chimney with a flashlight to make certain that the flue was shut tight and no skinny burglars could shimmy down like Santa Claus.

Then he'd hit the kitchen to sniff the stove for gas and stick his head in the oven, à la Sylvia Plath, to make sure there were no leaks.

Finally, into the bedrooms. He'd stick his schnozz right into my sleeping face to ascertain whether or not I was alive and breathing.

If I had the blanket pulled over my head, he'd slide the blanket back, lean close, and whisper, "Chris? Can you hear me? Are you awake? Are you breathing? Are you alive?" Till he succeeded in waking me up and—his face an inch from mine—scaring the shit out of me.

Then, satisfied that I was alive, he'd exit with a "Good night, Chris, sleep tight."

CABLE GUY

Dad could be paranoid.

Take something as simple as the cable company technician sent to our house to add a router or rewire a connection.

This really happened.

Dad and I had been out shopping. When we got home, the cable company truck was parked in our driveway.

"Chris, go inside and see where the cable guy is and come back out and tell me."

"Why?"

"I want to be able to get up to my room without him seeing me, recognizing me."

"Guess what, *schmuck*, he knows you live here."

"How would he know that?"

"Your name and address are on the fucking cable bill."

"Oh. Huh. Okay, well, I just don't wanna have to deal with him. You know, 'Ooh, Harvey Korman, can I have your autograph?'"

"Dad, every celebrity, every movie star in town has cable and has to deal with a cable guy coming to their house. With all due respect, you're not, like, Madonna or George Clooney or Barbra Streisand. The guy is not gonna hassle you for your autograph."

"Please."

I went inside. Sure enough, the cable guy was by the bar, splicing wires and stuff.

I went back out. "The coast is clear, Dad."

"Great. So I can get from the kitchen door up to my office without being seen?"

"Yes. But be careful. The guy looks a lot like Charles Manson. And he knows where you live."

THE GOUT

> FALSTAFF: A pox of this gout! or, a gout of this pox! For the one or the other plays the rogue with my great toe.
> *Henry IV, Part II*

Leave it to my father to come down with a Shakespearean disease, particularly one that plagued Shakespeare's most memorable comedic character.

His doctor had been clear: "Mr. Korman, cut out the drinking, the smoking, and the rich foods."

By "rich foods," I'm pretty sure he meant items like cheese blintzes and stuffed kishka from Nate'n Al.

"Dad, are you on medication?"

"It's complicated."

"Should you be drinking while you're on meds?"

He took another sip of his Bloody Mary. Dad not only loved Bloody Mary's, he was a master at concocting them, a true mixologist.

In reply to my question, Dad lit a cigarette.

"Didn't the doctor tell you to quit smoking?"

"Chris, I don't care. Tomorrow the gout may be worse, but I'll just deal with it."

"Dad—"

"—Chris, I'm seventy-nine. A tired old Jew. I want to drink and smoke."

BOOZE

Although Dad favored Bloody Mary's (Absolut was his go-to brand) if there was no tomato juice in the house, he'd opt for a vodka-on-the-rocks (Stoli) with a twist of lime.

Before bedtime at the end of long day, he'd pour himself a hefty Scotch. And there was always a shelf of Molson Gold in the fridge.

With Johnny Carson, a martini.

As Johnny famously said, "Happiness is when you're hungry, finding two olives in your martini."

THE BREAK-UP

By the tail end of 2007, Dad and Tim had been crisscrossing the country with their show for almost ten years, averaging 60-70 performances a year. That's a lot of travel and stress for two guys 80 years old.

They got tired of it.

And, maybe, tired of each other.

After all, they'd already been working together for over 40 years. Now, between coming up with fresh material, travel between dates, then the actual show, they were together 16-18 hours a day.

Maybe they started to get on each other's nerves. In any case, they called it a day.

TUMOR

One night in 2008, shortly after Dad's eighty-first birthday—February 15—he got out of bed and stood too quickly; he had a dizzy spell, fell, and hit his head on a credenza.

He was rushed to UCLA Medical Center.

At the hospital, they discovered that he had a brain tumor.

In retrospect, the tumor may have existed for most of his life. It could account for his behavior, in that he was always somewhat cranky. Everyone chalked it up to his being just another temperamental actor with wild mood swings.

In fact, he was often so dour that when he was on the *Carol Burnett Show*, Carol had a sign posted on his dressing room door that read: Mr. Happy-go-Lucky.

So maybe his dark moods were because of the damn tumor.

Were the doctors planning to operate, to try and remove the thing?

That became moot when, two days after the fall, he was in his office and experienced severe abdominal pain.

Back to the hospital, where it was discovered that he had a ruptured aortic aneurysm.

THE LONG ROAD

An aortic aneurysm is an abnormal bulge that occurs in the wall of the major blood vessel (aorta) that carries blood from your heart to your body.
https://www.mayoclinic.org/diseases-conditions/aortic-aneurysm/symptoms-causes/syc-20369472

When I heard Dad was in the hospital, UCLA Medical Center, I phoned Mom and told her I'd drive up to LA with Trish and Scott on the weekend.

"Chris, I'm sure Harvey would appreciate the thought, but please wait till he feels a little better."

"Really?"

"Really. He's asked me to tell his friends and family to give him a few days."

That sounded like my father; he didn't get sick often, but when he did, he only wanted to be left alone.

"Can I talk to him?"

"Unfortunately, he's got tubes in his nose and mouth. He can't do much more than nod, shake his head, or scribble a note."

I asked her to ask Maria when would be a good time to visit; a month or so later, I got the word and drove up from San Diego with Trish and Scott.

In Dad's hospital room, I confronted the worst sight I'd ever seen: He had IV tubes in both arms and, as Debbie had told me, a tube in his mouth, and oxygen tubes in his nostrils.

He couldn't speak, but the look in his eyes said, "Help me, Chris, I'm scared. I don't want to die."

I sat next to him. I felt absolutely helpless.

His doctor came in, checked the various machines Dad was hooked up to, and asked me if I could come back another time. Dad needed to rest.

I took the elevator down to the lobby, where I totally lost it. I crumpled to the floor and cried, bawled, sobbed. I felt like the worst son in the world because I couldn't comfort my father, let alone protect him from pain.

I had no conception of where I was or if there were people around, until a security guard came over and asked if I was okay.

At that point, I stood up, nodded, and headed out for the drive back to San Diego.

I didn't have a chance to visit again. On May 29, 2008, Dad passed.

CLOSE

In late 2007, well before the tumor and aneurysm diagnoses, Dad and I spoke on the phone.

We hadn't talked about my learning disability in years, so I'm not sure why it was on my mind, but I said, "Dad, you know, I always wondered how you felt about me being a constant burden on you, because of my issues."

"Chris, I've never thought of you as a burden, that's in your head, not mine. In my head, I'm just really proud of you, proud of the man you've become, proud of the husband and father you've become."

Wow.

After we spoke, I thought back on times we sat side-by-side on the couch to watch a baseball game or movie. Invariably, he'd put a protective arm around me and I'd rest my head on his shoulder or chest. This loving behavior went on well into my 20s and 30s.

He never believed that at some random age you become too embarrassed to show affection to your children.

THE SUN CITY THEATER COMPANY

I'm trying to start a theater company here in Las Vegas. There are four of us. The goal is to begin small, producing only two or three shows per year. Eventually, we will do longer runs but the important thing is to always be our own boss, to make our own decisions as to what shows we will produce, what actors, directors, and production people we will hire.

This enterprise, for me, will be far more rewarding than what I do on *TV Confidential*, in that I will have my hands directly on the wheel. And hopefully, there will be financial rewards that will benefit my family into the future.

Why start a theater company in a city that thrives on gambling and casino-style entertainment?

Because theater is a wonderful, inclusive environment; an opportunity to raise important topical issues and present them in an accessible entertaining manner.

From my perspective, people in the theater world tend to be more relaxed, more fun than people in the corporate/business world.

My associates want to call our company the Korman Players Theatre Troupe.

THE PURGE

The other day, Trish said to me, "Chris, for this book, celebrate what your father meant to you as a *Dad*. Tell funny stories about the two of you that his fans would love to hear—and which I've been hearing for 17 years. Unless you purge everything in your head about you and your father you're going to keep repeating those stores to everyone."

Okay, Trish, I'm purged.

THE ONLY TIME YOU FAIL IN LIFE IS WHEN YOU DON'T TRY

That was my father's motto, his mantra, his abiding testament; a rule he drove into my head at every appropriate moment. A rule I've tried to live by. It's the one piece of hand-me-down lore I won't purge from my head, even if it means spending eternity in a Heaven chock-a-block with actors who cross-dressed on television.

THE ONLY TIME YOU FAIL IN LIFE IS WHEN YOU DON'T TRY

Thanks, Dad!

ACKNOWLEDGEMENTS

My deepest thanks to those who made this book possible.

To my wife Patricia Korman and my son Scott Korman, from whom all blessings in my life flow.

To Bernie Furshpan, Ron Brawer, and Ben Ohmart for helping me with their patience, compassion, and sensitivity, to bring this project to fruition.

To my father, who gave me a rich tapestry of experiences, both personal and professional, to celebrate our lives together as a loving father and son.

To my sister, Maria, who shared with me these wonderful memories of Dad that we both cherish and keep in our hearts.

To my mother, my cheerleader. Thank you for bestowing on me the greatest gift a child can be given—unconditional love.

www.ingramcontent.com/pod-product-compliance
Lightning Source LLC
Chambersburg PA
CBHW050111170426
43198CB00014B/2536